THE
OVERTONE
EFFECT

THE
OVERTONE
EFFECT

Live
Your Life
on a High Note!

JAN CARLEY

Author of *Harmony from the Inside Out*

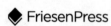 FriesenPress

Suite 300 - 990 Fort St
Victoria, BC, V8V 3K2
Canada
www.friesenpress.com

Published by: Creative Coaching Group Publishing
775 Sawyer's Lane
Vancouver, B.C. V5Z 3Z8
CANADA

Legal deposit, Library and Archives Canada, 2017

Distributed to the trade by The Ingram Book Company

To my mother, Mig,
who supported everyone in their dreams
and who always believed in mine

CONTENTS

INTRODUCTION

I t was at a weekly chorus rehearsal, while standing on the risers in an old wooden community hall on a hot summer's night, that I first heard and felt the thrilling, goosebump-producing sensation of a musical overtone.

My passion is singing a cappella barbershop harmony with the award-winning Lions Gate Chorus, a group associated with Sweet Adelines International, the largest worldwide singing organization for women. In the barbershop art form, overtones are created when a singer, or a group of singers, achieve precisely the right type of tuning in the notes they sing. That magical balance of sound frequencies creates extra notes that can be heard - *yet are not actually being sung!* Those extra notes are overtones. Overtones are the chocolate éclairs of the barbershop world – once you have had one, you want another. In those moments of singing in the midst of overtones, all feels right with the world.

Having experienced this phenomenon, it made sense that I would use the musical metaphor of an overtone to describe a transcendent state or a place that results from all parts of one's life being in complete alignment and harmony. While living in your overtone, your signature brilliance has an impact far greater than what is seen on the surface. An organization, when feeling the Overtone Effect, becomes even more than the sum of its parts. In that overtone place, an undeniable universal energy and force has been created that is beyond what is seemingly possible.

As I coach more and more individuals and teams, I realize that what people want is a focused road to lead them to their place of highest potential – their overtone. This inspired me to create an easy-to-follow system that leads the reader from A to Z. The overtone system in this book can be applied to any individual, organization, team, or community to which you belong.

I use it worldwide with my individual clients, corporate teams, and choral organizations. The Lions Gate Chorus has been my guinea pig for this inner mastery coaching work. The overtone approach has supported them in rising to, and consistently staying in, the Top Five standings at the International Chorus Competition since 2007.

As leaders of companies, choruses, and non-profit community groups, we must change to keep in stride with what is wanted and needed by our employees, members, and volunteers. Those changes require a shift in our approach from a "fixed" position to a "generative" one if we expect to grow and thrive in a sustainable way into the future.

No matter what your corporate or community focus, *The Overtone Effect* will help you make that shift. And yes, it all starts with you.

What is it going to take to find your overtone? Simply read this book through the lens of possibility that this system creates. Do the Reflection Exercises in each chapter. Stay curious. To dive even deeper, purchase the companion *Overtone Effect Workbook* (details on the back page.) The workbook is a comprehensive 70-page compilation of exercises to help you and your team apply the overtone system.

My hope is that this book will give you a system to follow and the tools you need to kick-start your culture revitalization, whether it be a personal one or an organizational group culture shift. Along the way, may you all feel the Overtone Effect!

SECTION ONE
Beginning the Overtone Conversation

Chapter 1
WHAT IS AN OVERTONE?

As I noted in the Introduction, a passion of mine is singing four-part a cappella harmony in the style known as barbershop. In that popular art form, overtones are created when a singer or group of singers achieve precisely the right type of tuning in the notes they sing. That intricate balance of sound frequencies creates the natural phenomenon of overtones, which are extra notes that can be heard, *yet are not actually being sung.* In barbershop harmony singing, we all are consistently working to achieve a balance and alignment of sound and tone so we can achieve musical overtones together. Finding them may be difficult, and sometimes fleeting, but when created they can easily cause physical responses such as extreme goosebumps and a thrilling feeling deep in our core. It's what we live for in barbershop harmony!

Using the metaphor of a musical overtone, imagine aligning all parts of your life or all facets of your organization in perfect harmony to get results greater than what you thought were possible! Something greater than the sum of its parts. An extra note. An overtone. Every individual, team, community group, and organization has the capacity to create and feel the Overtone Effect.

Amanda is a member of the False Creek Racing Canoe Club Dragon Boat team, winners of three gold medals at the 2014 World Club crew championships in Italy. With twenty paddlers in the forty-foot boat, two abreast, teamwork is imperative. Though everyone has the same stroke, each person in the boat plays a different role. In the intense two-minute race, all paddlers need to be in perfect synch both when paddles are in the air and in the water. When that happens, the front of the boat rises up and lifts off the waves. The whole boat feels light and like it is levitating. Amanda describes it as an immensely satisfying and magical feeling. It's the dragon boating overtone.

It is even possible (though more difficult) for individuals to create a musical overtone all by themselves. As you will discover in the chapters on personal mastery, we start with the work of creating our own individual overtone and then expand and connect it with others to amplify the Overtone Effect.

Canadian Shannon Harris[1] is a two-time International Gold Medal Barbershop Quartet Champion, singing the foundational bass part. Shannon sings with such aligned vocal production that she regularly creates an overtone all by herself.

She describes the feeling: "When I sing with absolute lift, resonance and maximum space – with no tension – it allows for continual movement of the sound. It feels like there is no cap on the sound I can produce and the sensation is one of total freedom. I can actually feel vibrations of sound coming out of my eyes." Notice the several different elements that Shannon needs to have in total alignment in order to produce her overtone. She says that with even one of those elements absent, the overtone is gone, or in her words, "squashed." Yet when all are in alignment, she feels "total freedom."

You may have felt this in your life. When everything is so totally aligned you feel effortlessly transported to that "sweet spot" or "zone" where you feel at your best and get your greatest results with ease.

I once felt this when singing in competition onstage with my quartet, *Fandango*. I was completely present in the moment and acutely aware of my own breath and the sounds my voice was making, yet I was also *outside* myself observing my performance as if it was happening to someone else. My being, my essence, was perfectly aligned with my actions. It was a most unusual calming and freeing feeling. In that moment, I had found my performance overtone.

Perhaps you have experienced the Overtone Effect with a group, such as when your work together is aligned and transports you to live into possibilities without limits.

Deb described working as the General Merchandising Manager in the head office of a huge membership warehouse club in the early 90s. They had just done a history-making mammoth merger with another warehouse giant and needed to adapt and work in a new way so that they could capitalize on their doubled buying power. How could they turn the merger and the resulting changes that were sure to be disruptive into something that worked for the staff team and the company?

Deb said they adopted a rallying cry of "Synergy!" This cry was single-focused and aligned with their vision and goals. It connected with the corporate values and core focus, and was crystal clear to the entire staff. The conversations shifted from fear or annoyance at the impact of the changes to excitement that their buying power had doubled in size. They began thinking about how they could capitalize on that to help their members (customers). It took about four years for them to fully transition and live into their corporate overtone of "synergy," and since then the company has been enjoying immense annual profits.

When you are working in your overtone you can create amazing results, and go where you only dreamed of going.

REFLECTION OPPORTUNITY

Many chapters will include a Reflection Opportunity, a series of questions that builds on the chapter content. The reflection questions are designed to provoke thought and insight. I recommend you take the time to let your ideas percolate. Reflect alone or with a friend or support person. If you have a notebook to write down your thoughts, the learning will be embedded further.

For further exploration, the companion 70-page *Overtone Effect Workbook* has extensive detailed exercises and worksheets building on the book's concepts. See back page for purchase details.

Experiencing an Overtone

1. Have you ever felt the sensation of an overtone in your life, in your work, in your relationships? A time when you or your team was transported beyond what seemed on the surface to be possible? If so, what do you remember about the experience?

2. If not, what do you imagine it might feel like to feel the Overtone Effect?

Chapter 2
HOW TO CREATE AN OVERTONE

I was honored to hear the Dalai Lama speak in Vancouver at a sold-out event in the 50,000-seat BC Place Stadium. At the end of his talk he asked for questions, and someone way up in the nosebleed section of the bleachers asked: "How can we create peace in the world?"

The Dalai Lama paused and then answered with conviction: "You can't."

There was a shocked hush in the stadium. You could have heard a pin drop. After a long pause, the Dalai Lama went on to explain: "You can't create peace in the world. You can create peace in yourself. And once you have created peace in yourself ... then turn to your family – create peace in your family. And once there is peace in your family ... turn to your neighbors. Once there is peace with your neighbors, turn to your community ... and so on. Always begin within."

The Dalai Lama's message can be applied as we start working to create our own overtone. Although we might be inclined to look externally to access something to help create that magical state, instead we must work from the inside out and start with who we "be." Rather than asking, "What can we *do* to create our overtone?" ask "Who can we *be*?"

Happily, not only is who we *be* the most important part of our overtone journey, it is also the one thing we have control over. We get to choose what and who we want to be.

So much of our focus in life is put on our almighty "To Do" lists; yet, the real meaning of life is not in the doing. Author Neale Donald Walsch[1] said, "We are human beings, not human doings." In fact, I would go so far as to say that our "doing-ness" has become our "undoing." If we **DO** "**x**" we will **HAVE** *"x"* and then we will **BE** *"x."* For example: "After I get through university, I will get a job and then I will be fulfilled" *or* "If we work hard, we can buy a house and then we will be happy" *or* "Once this busy period at work is over I will have more time and then I will be less stressed out." We forget to live in the present moment and an overtone only exists in the present moment.

An overtone only exists in the present moment.

Switch to Be-Do-Have

Changing our formula for living is a simple flip of the words from Do-Have-Be to Be-Do-Have.

First and most important is who we *Be* – which inspires the *Do* – with the *Have* then being the result. We are on this earth to *be* something, possibly even many things. We are here to live and contribute in this moment. If you are intentional about how you *be* in each moment you will change how you think, then change how you feel and what actions you take. As a result, the world around you will change.

An overtone is created by a magical balance of elements. Each element contributes. In our discussion of balance (See Chapter 24) we see it is not a matter of managing your time or giving equal effort to two opposing sides, it is about aligning your behavior with what is really important to you.

Once you fully tap into who you *be*, what you do must align with that "being." Balance and alignment of all elements are key to creating an overtone. This gets even more complex with an organization, as every building block must be in place for the overtone to be created and sustained. With even a slight wobble or one shaky foundational brick, the ability to create an overtone will be compromised.

An overtone for an organization cannot be imposed from the outside in. An overtone is also more difficult to create if there are some naysayers in the group. Ideally, everyone will be willing to show up and do the work together no matter what their level of comfort. Working together in perfect alignment creates a new possibility.

I do a lot of work with high-performing teams and was dumbfounded when coaching Gavin, a CFO who protested and resisted the leadership development work I was doing with him and his team. He said to me, "I'm old (55!); I'm set in my ways. I'm not at work to be happy. There's too much to do. I'm here to do my job. I don't need to be in my sweet spot."

He was non-apologetic and unwavering in his commitment to remain exactly where he was. I persisted with my exploration of his situation, and found his resistance was based on two factors: 1) being overwhelmed at the scope of his responsibilities; and 2) having a fear of failure. Though my work with him did not last long enough to bring him fully onboard with the rest of the team, he was willing to entertain the possibility that some changes might benefit his colleagues and that was a big priority for him. Even in that limited way, he was enrolled in change, which meant the team could move forward.

If you are willing to be all-in to the process of your overtone journey, I guarantee you won't be disappointed. The journey may be winding, with some rough sections, but it will be worth it.

REFLECTION OPPORTUNITY

Leave your judge's hat aside and approach this assessment as a neutral fact-finding identification. This is merely the starting point of your journey.

Willingness Meter

1. How willing are you (on a scale of 1–10) to go on the overtone journey?
2. If you're not at 10, what's in the way?
3. What do you need to help shift your number closer to 10?

Readiness Meter

1. How ready are you (on a scale of 1–10) for the overtone journey?
2. What do you need to help shift your readiness number closer to 10?
3. Who/What can support you?

Overtone System

SECTION TWO
The Overtone Approach

GENERATIVE:
Having the power or function of generating, originating, producing or reproducing.

The Overtone approach is a generative process. It builds on the popular positivity approach that was integral to my first book, *Harmony from the Inside Out,* and has succeeded in changing the working atmosphere of groups I have worked with over the past ten years. The Overtone approach goes a step further to actually generate and create action.

The Overtone approach will actively transport you, your team, and your organization to a new and expansive world of possibility and opportunity.

THE OVERTONE APPROACH

MOVING THOUGHT **TO ACTION**

Checklist:

✓ Generative Focus

✓ Generative Mindset

✓ Generative Language

Chapter 3
GENERATIVE FOCUS

**A generative focus liberates potential
and leverages our capacity to create,
learn, and produce desired results.**

For the past several years, I have been espousing the value of positive thinking and working in all of my coaching programs. In particular, with the high-performance a cappella performance groups I coach worldwide, I have discovered how positivity creates a more joyful environment. Residual effects spill over in increased performance excellence, unity, team effectiveness, and individual happiness. By focusing the brain on desired outcomes and possibilities (instead of current weaknesses and flaws) there is more capacity for learning and insight.

Choral groups have benefited hugely by adopting a strengths-based focus and turning their rehearsal hall into a "Positivity Zone." Positivity sparks possibility, expansion, and abundance, whereas negativity keeps us in a frozen state of scarcity and lack. Nurturing a positive mental state has proven critical to achieving positive performance results.

In world-renowned researcher Dr. Barbara Fredrickson's seminal work on positivity, she outlines the research that shows the role of positive emotions in the development and maintenance of human flourishing. Fredrickson says that "to flourish means to live within an optimal range of human functioning, one that connotes goodness, generativity, growth, and resilience." Human flourishing goes beyond happiness in that it encompasses both feeling good and doing good. With regard to optimal amounts of positivity, mathematical ratios have given way to the statement "higher is better, within bounds."[1]

As we will see in this overtone work, the results are not just accidental. There is now a considerable body of science backing up the benefits of positive psychology concepts.

> *"Positive emotions flood our brains with dopamine and serotonin, chemicals that not only make us feel good, but dial up the learning centers of our brains to higher levels. They help us organize new information, keep that information in the brain longer, and retrieve it faster later on."* [2]
> -Shawn Achor, *The Happiness Advantage*

Performance potential can be enhanced by using mental techniques such as affirmations, power thoughts, visualization, positive self-talk, learning how to flip focus, reducing mental interference, and acknowledging what is working. Being positive, it seems, is a very good thing.

Going Beyond Positive

In any high-performance organization, whether it is a cappella choral singing, elite athletics, or a corporation or non-profit organization with high ideals and standards, focusing and building on what is right is the key to moving forward. Instead, many groups focus almost exclusively on what needs to be fixed. I have encountered some misunderstandings and resistance to fully embracing the positivity concept in many of the performance groups with which I work.

Many voice concerns that positivity means ignoring the things that aren't working and that by not being real or truthful it could inhibit forward progress to technical mastery. "If we focus on the good stuff, how does the stuff that is wrong get fixed?" they ask. "If we don't mention what is wrong and work on it, then aren't we lying to ourselves by telling only half the story?"

Let's get this super clear: Being positive does not mean we should walk around with rose-colored glasses ignoring what is wrong and glossing over problems. If positivity is a platitude, then it can actually be negative.

We must not ignore current reality. We must fully acknowledge where we are now (without judgment) and then shift our thinking to generate ways to strategically move into what we want, where we want to go, and how we can get there. The generative overtone approach takes us from a positive mental state into dynamic, life-giving action.

Where It All Began

The generative approach is based on the principles of an organizational development model called "Appreciative Inquiry"[3] pioneered by Professors David Cooperrider and Suresh Srivastva in the 1980s, and described in my 2009 book, *Harmony from the Inside Out*. "Appreciative Inquiry (AI) is an exciting way to embrace organizational change. Its assumption is simple: Every organization has something that works right – things that give it life when it is most alive, effective, successful, and connected in healthy ways to its stakeholders and communities. AI begins by identifying what is positive and connecting to it in ways that heighten energy and vision for change."[4]

The approach also embraces making a shift in how we look at individuals – be they colleagues, partners, offspring, or fellow chorus members. "Appreciative Inquiry deliberately seeks to discover people's exceptionality – their unique gifts, strengths, and qualities. It actively searches and recognizes people for their specialties – their essential contributions and achievements. Appreciative Inquiry builds momentum and success because it believes in people. It really is an invitation to a positive revolution."[5]

Most of us have been taught, trained, and rewarded for using a problem-solving approach; that is, to look for what isn't working, figure out what the problem is, analyze it, and then think up ways to fix the problem and put an action plan in place to do so. The problem-solving approach is a deficit-based approach that focuses on looking back and correcting. That approach works well for linear processes such as finding the error in a financial spreadsheet – and in situations where something is either right or it's wrong, and there can be no shades of gray in between. However, the problem-solving approach doesn't foster creating and learning because it supports tunnel thinking. In addition, there can be a cognitive shutdown when we focus on what's wrong. A generative approach would have us build from strengths, identify what we want, and imagine and create what could be. Then we can implement action that leads us toward a new possibility.

The generative overtone approach takes us from a positive mental state into dynamic, life-giving action.

Do you have to be positive to be generative? The short answer is "yes." To clarify – you don't need to be positive; you just can't be negative to be generative. Being negative keeps us stuck and is non-generative. However, being positive on its own is not generative – it is the *result* of being positive that makes something generative. For example: "That is a good idea" is positive; "That is a good idea and I see how I could use it to move us into new markets" is generative.

Five Key Steps to Support a Generative Focus

1. Identify and Acknowledge Reality

To think generatively and create new ideas and possibilities we must start by acknowledging (without judgment) the current reality or situation. **Be real and be aware of the facts.** Once the awareness is there, shift your focus. Rather than remaining focused on the lack, or the problem, move to Step 2 and begin to think generatively toward the future or conditions you want. Then watch the possibilities open up.

2. Think Generatively

Volkart May[6] is a large professional contact center in the United States to which companies outsource inside sales business. The company has found over time that it is very difficult to staff the center with full-time people. Forty hours per week on the phone is very fatiguing, and they found that with full-time staff, either performance fell off or people just burned out.

As a consequence, almost all of their staff is part-time, working twenty-five to thirty hours per week. Most of these folks do something else during their off hours. They have lots of employees who are going to school part-time; they have a photographer, a real estate agent, a bartender, an interior designer, and teachers who work during the summer. They allow people to work whatever hours they prefer during business hours of 7:00AM to 7:00PM, so long as they work a minimum of twenty-five hours per week.

Their management team has consistently had issues with this staffing process. The system is chaotic and hard to manage. There might be lots of staff at one time of day, and very few later on. Schedules are constantly changing as callers adjust to kids' activities, class timetables, and life in general. The management team has been wrestling with how to schedule their employees in a more conventional way.

When they made a small mental shift and started thinking about the situation generatively they came up with questions: What is good about this situation? What competitive advantage does this give us? What might happen if we embraced the chaos of this flexible system?

Their answers surprised them and created a shift in their feelings toward the system. It turns out that the chaotic scheduling is often an advantage to the company. Many employees love the flexibility and as a result, retention of these part-time callers is high. The sales division uses the fact that Volkart May's part-time callers are always fresh and energetic as a selling point to get new clients.

Once they embraced their system, it became an asset, not a liability. A shift in focus proved to be a positive business differentiator for them.

The one question you must always ask yourself is: **"Is this thought generative?"** Does it open possibilities? Can it move me or the situation forward? If not, reframe and ask yourself some generative mindset questions. Notice the mental space that opens up when you begin to think generatively.

3. Focus Toward

One easy way to understand a generative focus is through the legend of the two wolves.

> A grandfather sitting with his grandchildren told them, "In every life there is a terrible fight – a fight between two wolves. One wolf is evil: he is fear, anger, envy, greed, arrogance, self-pity, resentment, and deceit. The other wolf is good: joy, serenity, humility, confidence, generosity, truth, gentleness, and compassion."
> A child asked, "Grandfather, which wolf will win?"
> The grandfather looked the child in the eye and said, "The one you feed."

Continue to **focus and refocus your energy on the result or conditions you want**, instead of focusing on what you don't want. Acting generatively will inspire you to move *toward* a solution instead of moving *away* from a problem.[7] When examining a situation, or working to better it, approach your planning from a generative perspective. Feel the momentum that surges as a result.

4. Speak Generatively

This is an area so critical I wrote a complete chapter about it (Chapter 5). One word can shut a person's mind down. When you speak, **listen to your words – are they generative**? Or do your words keep you (or others) standing still?

> Louise is a professional workplace mediator who successfully approaches conflict-ridden, high-emotion mediation conversations with a generative focus. Though it would be easy for dialogue to center solely on the problems that bring her clients to the point of engaging a mediator, she begins the process by taking the client(s) beyond the immediate issue that brought them into the room. She encourages them to go beyond themselves, to imagine and then to speak generatively about their desired future state, in order to give them perspective from which to approach the matter at hand. Speaking from a place of what they want frames the dialogue in a way that can help both parties come to a mutually-satisfying solution.

5. Listen Generatively

Most often in conversation we listen with the intent of formulating a response. With a slight shift in focus, generative listening would have us **listen with the intent to understand.** Global consultant and MIT lecturer, C. Otto Scharmer, goes further and says that generative listening actually connects us to something larger than ourselves, and in essence we then start listening from *"the emerging field of future possibility."*[8] Imagine that!

REFLECTION OPPORTUNITY

<u>Create a Generative Brain Break</u>

(Time needed: 2–3 minutes)

The concept of these "G" moments is to give the brain an opportunity to refocus to an appreciative approach that moves us into a "toward" mental state. Pick a question to ask yourself, offer one out for a two-minute break in a team meeting, or pose one to your singers in the middle of a rehearsal.

- What could positively shift my/your/our thinking about the current situation?
- What are the opportunities here? (Versus focusing on a problem, weakness or lack)
- How could I/we change our perspective?
- Where could I/we grow?
- What is going well right now?
- What could I/we improve next time?
- What do I/we need for support?
- What is working now that I/we could expand on?
- What do I/we know about…? How can I/we apply that?
- What would I/you like to take away from this meeting/rehearsal? Etc.
- What is a new way of looking at this?
- What are the possibilities here?
- What will I/you do differently next time?

FLIP YOUR FOCUS – WHAT DO YOU WANT?

Sometimes the simplest of concepts can be the most profound. We study complex organizational development theories. We read endless personal development books seeking nuggets of enlightenment. We take courses and go on retreats in our continual search for ways to make our lives and organizations the best they can be. Yet there is a dead simple two-word concept that you can adopt today that will forever change your life. Write these two words on your bulletin board. Keep them handy: **Flip it!**

We create our reality by what we choose to focus on. A generative approach focused on what we have and what we want will open up possibilities and move us forward to achieving our overtone. The same principle applies to our mindset. **Where thought goes, energy flows.**

The Flip it Concept

Consider your current thoughts about a personal or work situation. Are you thinking of the struggle, the lack, the what-is-not-working?

If you are, flip your thinking and shift your thoughts to your desired state. Turn your focus to the abundant possibilities. Watch your energy shift when you Flip it!

> E.g. Your focus: I don't have any work lined up for next month.
> (While mentally focused there, you are stuck with no work.)
> Flip it: I want to get three more clients next month.
> (That opens you up to the next step: Ok, that's what I want; now how will I achieve it?)

> Board Meeting focus: Sales are flat for our gala event. No one is buying tickets. We are going to lose a lot of money.
> (While energy is focused there, no tickets are sold.)
> Flip it: We need to sell two hundred more tickets to break even.
> (Opens up to the next step: Okay, now how can we do that?)

When any of my coaching clients start to focus on their problems (i.e. what isn't working), I see them quickly losing energy. My job then becomes managing the coaching session to make sure they rise out of their downward spiral.

Alana, a successful senior VP in a busy, high-stress tech environment, came to me with a non-stop litany of the things in her life that were causing her current state of complete overwhelm. After Alana had exhausted her download, rather than stay with her in that state, I acknowledged how she was feeling and then asked a simple question, "Imagine yourself being totally on top of things, organized and in charge – how does that feel?" That flipped her focus and took her to a future state, where she was in control, calm, and relaxed. It had the effect of opening up possibilities for her in a situation that had seemed hopeless minutes earlier.

Remember: By keeping our minds in a *toward* state we can more easily promote growth and insight. We experience resistance when we try to work *away* from something.

REFLECTION OPPORTUNITY

<u>Flip It!</u>

Think of a situation in any part of your life where there is a gap between where you are and where you want to be.

1. Spend a couple of minutes focusing on the gap and what is missing. If you are doing this reflection in a group, engage in a group discussion about what is lacking.

2. Now consciously "Flip Your Focus" and put your attention to what will close the gap. Focus your group discussion on what you need or want – your desired state.

3. What happened when you "Flipped It?"

USING THE GENERATIVE <u>SOAR</u> APPROACH WITH YOUR ORGANIZATION

Many of you will have participated in SWOT analyses in group strategic planning sessions in which you look at your organization's **S**- Strengths, **W**-Weaknesses, **O**- Opportunities and **T**- Threats. The challenge with a SWOT exercise is that discussion often tends to concentrate on the weaknesses and threats. The negative energy takes over and draws focus.

The generative Appreciative Inquiry approach calls for a new acronym for our work – instead of SWOT, use **SOAR**.[9] The shift to a SOAR acronym (**S**- Strengths, **O**- Opportunities, **A**- Aspirations, **R**- Results) will expand your creative space and possible outcomes. What formerly was labeled a **W**-Weakness is now an **O**- Opportunity for growth and change. **A**- Aspirations focus on identifying your and your organization's deepest desires and determining what you *really* want. And **R**- Results is, of course, is the realization of those desires.

You can use the SOAR concept as a generative planning tool and mental quick-shifter for any team or organization.

Region 6 of Sweet Adelines International[10] covers a vast geographical area ranging from Manitoba and Northern Ontario, Canada, to North and South Dakota, Minnesota, Wisconsin and parts of Iowa. The Region includes twenty choruses and over 635 singers. In an '*Overtone Effect*' workshop with the Region's Leadership, the group identified the wide geographical spread of membership as one of the biggest challenges for regional unity and forward motion.

With SWOT, that might be considered a weakness, but I turned their discussion to a generative focus using the SOAR concept, asserting that every weakness is an opportunity for growth or change. I asked what the unique opportunities might be for such a sweeping geographic region. The energy in the room changed from defeat to optimism!

The group quickly saw the benefits of being able to have a greater impact on more communities and began brainstorming innovative opportunities to increase communication, with new out-of-the-box methods to keep in touch and better serve their membership.

REFLECTION OPPORTUNITY

Shifting to SOAR

Think of a weakness or challenge you are having with your team or organization. What is the opportunity there?

Chapter 4
GENERATIVE MINDSET

Lesley-Ann was perched confidently on her mountain bike at the top of Ned's Atomic Dustbin – a treacherous mountain bike trail on Vancouver's North Shore Mountains. Legend has it that the trail was named for a legendary rider named Ned who was reduced to dust at the bottom of the mountain by the ferocity of the ride. Lesley-Ann was on a date with Derek, an avid biker who had not yet conquered this particular run. As he looked down at the intimidating black diamond run before them, he asked, "How the heck are we going to get down there? All I see are trees." Lesley-Ann looked at him in incredulous wonder. "Really?" she said. "All I see is the path."

Neuroscience tells us that how we focus attention shapes the structures in our brain. Lesley-Ann was harnessing the automatic mechanism of the reticular activating system (RAS) of the brain to bring relevant information to her attention. The RAS can't distinguish between reality and fiction. It believes the messages we are telling it. Therefore, by visualizing a very specific picture from her conscious mind of the path she wanted, she sent an exact message to her RAS. The RAS passed it along to her subconscious mind and literally helped her to *see* the path.

What we tell ourselves to focus on is what we will see.

Athletes use the power of the subconscious all the time. Golf superstar Jason Day incorporates a visualization process before every golf shot he takes. During his pre-shot routine he closes his eyes and imagines the shot he wants. He does this to still his conscious mind. For an elite athlete, it's the subconscious mind that drives the performance.

One's physical skill for a task is acquired through conscious repetition. But when you're swinging the club during a round, the conscious mind has to be kept quiet. When you try too hard, your conscious mind overrides the subconscious, and performance suffers. All players at the top level of professional golf are capable of playing the shots required to win, but it's how successful they are in managing the generative mental game that makes the pivotal difference.

Your Brain Can Change

We can't discuss shifting to an overtone mindset without talking about the phenomenal generative capacity of our brains. Interest in the field of neuroscience has exploded over the past couple of decades, and amazing discoveries are being made almost daily. Neuroscience is the study of the nervous system - including the brain, spinal cord, and networks of nerve cells called neurons - with a focus on its relation to behavior and learning. One of the biggest discoveries is the concept of neuroplasticity. Research shows that aspects of the brain have the capacity to change with learning (plasticity) and to create changes in our neural connections (neuroplasticity).

Neuroscientist Michael M. Merzenich, PhD, at the University of California explains that, "the brain is not like a computer that has fixed wiring and connections. Every aspect of you is created by the brain revising itself in response to your interactions in the world. How you define yourself – the person you are – is a product of plastic changes in your brain."[1]

We now know that it is possible to rewire our brains, and change preset patterns by building new neural pathways. The implication for the field of personal development is huge.

This is an exciting concept when thinking about creating our overtone. Our minds can create what we want to create. The idea of accessing or experiencing something greater than what currently exists is entirely possible.

HOW TO ADOPT A GENERATIVE MINDSET

Develop a Growth Mindset

World-renowned psychologist Dr. Carol Dweck offers groundbreaking insights in her book, *Mindset – The New Psychology of Success.*[2] In it she writes about the differences between the limiting "fixed mindset" and the expansive "growth mindset."

In a fixed mindset you believe that basic qualities, such as intelligence and talent, are fixed traits, and you spend your life proving those traits. In this kind of mindset you believe that talent is what creates success, and you're likely to have an internal monologue that is quite judgmental. Because you are focused on being good at all times, you are constantly judging how you have fared.

In a growth mindset you believe that your basic ability can be improved through dedication and hard work, and that talent and brains are merely the starting point. A growth mindset is focused on getting better, on improvement and developing skills so that you perform better than you did before. A growth mindset aids in expanding creativity, innovation, resiliency, and performance potential.

Adopting a growth mindset is generative, and key to achieving an overtone.

REFLECTION OPPORTUNITY

1. In what parts of your life and work is your mindset fixed, and in what parts do you regularly adopt a growth mindset?

2. What might happen if you considered a growth mindset in those areas where your mindset is now fixed?

Show Up as a Learner

As a Type A adult learner enrolled in Royal Roads University's Executive Coaching Program,[3] I was being hard on myself when I hadn't mastered all of the coaching fundamentals by day two of the course residency. When I expressed my distress to Master Certified Coach Scott Richardson, one of the core faculty, he asked, "Jan, what will it take for you to show up as a learner in this program?" That stopped me dead in my tracks and I instantly felt relieved. "Hey," I thought, "I'm not expected to know it all – I am a learner." The freedom and liberation I felt at not having to know it all was transformational.

A generative mindset is a learner mindset. When we show up as a learner, we are in effect saying we do not know everything; that we are open and willing to grow. How to do it? Simple – *stay curious*. We remind ourselves of this as professional coaches all the time. The second we stop being curious, and exercise our "knowing muscle" we close possibilities for our clients.

Open up your world and your thinking by actively showing up as a learner in everything you do. Seek knowledge. Feel the pressure lift and the space open up when you relieve yourself of the burden of having to know everything. We are here as students of life – constantly learning.

When you don't show up as a learner it ends possibility, limits your options and closes in your world. As soon as you think you know it all, you atrophy. If you remain curious and open to whatever life brings, you will have a greater possibility of finding your overtone.

There is no end to the mastery continuum that we can set for our lives.

REFLECTION OPPORTUNITY

Be a Learner

1. In what situations could you benefit from the liberation of not having to know it all?
2. What might it feel like to show up as a learner?
3. How does a conversation change when you go into it with a mindset of curiosity?

Move from Judge to Assessor

You know the feeling. You are in the middle of a presentation to your regional staff team and it seems to be going well. You have prepared for months and know your stuff. Suddenly, your boss walks in and stands at the back of the room with her arms crossed. A thought pops into your head: *Oh no, what is she doing here?* You fumble your next sentence. Another thought runs through your head: *You idiot – you are screwing up. Your boss is going to think you are useless.* You start to sweat. You get through the presentation. People shake your hand and say, "Great stuff." Although you smile and thank them, all you are thinking is how you screwed up when your boss walked in.

Sound familiar? Your inner judge has pounded the gavel and sentenced you harshly. You can't even hear the praise of your colleagues. Your inner judge has rendered his or her decision: *You blew it!*

The crippling and limiting negative effects of self-judgment is a theme I see consistently in my high-achieving corporate clients. It is also a debilitating theme that rears its ugly head in a dramatic way as my performance clients head into their singing competitions.

A judgment is a black and white statement of criticism that implies a good or bad labeling of one's value or worth. Most often our inner judge delivers a negative verdict, and we end up feeling bad about ourselves. A judgment rarely has the effect of making us feel better or moving us into being more successful. In fact, it usually has the opposite effect, and can undermine us in a nanosecond as in the previous example. A judgment implies a gavel coming down hard with the verdict rendered.

To move into a more generative state that will create new possibilities, we must shift from self-judgment to self-assessment. Self-assessment is an objective process that doesn't support or categorize a good or bad point of view. It simply notices and evaluates. We then move toward constructing the state or condition we want – toward our personal overtone.

The judge is reactive; an assessor is a learner who can be responsive. An assessment creates freedom and future possibilities for learning, whereas a judgment often closes the door. An assessment keeps the sense of our personal value separate from the evaluation of our functioning or actions. Instead of a judgment of worth, make an evaluation or assessment of what *is*.

Four Steps to Move from Judge to Assessor

1. **Notice:** Awareness is the first step. Let's use the example in the previous story and work through these steps like it's happening now. So – you simply become aware that your self-judge is getting louder after your boss walks in.

2. **Observe:** As you notice your self-judge turning up the volume, adopt the cool calmness of an outside observer. The great Boston Philharmonic conductor Benjamin Zander advises his musician students to replace their judging thoughts with observation, smile, and then say, "How fascinating!"[4] In this example, you might think, "How fascinating that the sight of my boss is causing me to lose confidence."

3. **Shift to a Balanced Assessment:** After becoming aware of your inner judge, shift your focus to a balanced assessment of the situation. You might think: "What is really happening here? I am well prepared. Until my boss walked in, people were engaged and enjoying the material." If your inner judge persists, firmly acknowledge him/her and think, "It is not productive to talk to me in the middle of my speech so I will get back to you later." Give yourself permission to keep the learning to the post-event reflection. There's lots of time for that!

4. **Reflect Post-Event:** In your post-event reflection, keep to objective evaluation. Think about how you want to improve the next time; draw on your past experience of success, and move into the future from a place of strength and possibility.

REFLECTION OPPORTUNITY

Experiment with the four steps by using an example from your life.

Step 1 Notice: (What is happening?)

Step 2 Become the Observer: (How fascinating that…)

Step 3 Shift to Assessment: (What is really happening here?)

Step 4 Reflect: (Stay objective. How can I improve next time?)

Be Intentional

A generative mindset is an intentional one. A random thought can go anywhere, but intention is purpose-filled. An overtone doesn't just happen by chance. We are the only thinkers in our own minds, and practicing active intention is a powerful reinforcement of the conditions we want.

> *"An intention activates neurons in your brain by sending signals from one neuron to another and that alerts your whole being. Going even further than that, your neurons send signals that go beyond your body that resonate at your own unique frequency. Your resonance connects you with the Universal energy field...your intention sets everything in motion to influence events so they are aligned with your thoughts."* [5]
> —Dr. Adam McLeod, special focus in integrative oncology

REFLECTION OPPORTUNITY

Experiment with being intentional while doing a routine task such as eating a bowl of cereal. Perform that routine task with mental purpose. Notice with conscious thought every part of your routine from the stretch of your arm to get the bowl out of the cupboard, to the feel of cold air as you take the milk out of the fridge, to the weight of the spoon as you raise it to your mouth, to the texture of the cereal, to the taste and feeling of chewing, to swallowing.

What did you notice about that experiment?

How did that routine experience change when you were intentional about it?

Experiment with other parts of your life. How might it feel being intentional in a conversation with your partner? In an activity?

Chapter 5
GENERATIVE LANGUAGE

Communicating with language is a big responsibility – we speak an average of up to 15,000 words per day. Understanding the effect of language and being more intentional about the words you use could be the most pivotal thing you can do to help create an overtone.

Initially, I thought the language piece would be the easiest part of this overtone work to embrace, yet I have found for most people shifting language is a big stumbling block. Of course, viewed through a generative lens, stumbling blocks are always areas for potential growth!

Our language patterns and mental foci have been deeply imprinted since birth by all of our life influencers – parents, teachers, friends, and experiences – and it takes persistence and commitment to shift. Finding and maintaining one's overtone is not a static endeavor. Much as the world around us is changing, so we must continually open ourselves up to growth and new learning.

Even a single word in a sentence has the power to shift our intended meaning from generative and forward-moving to stalling or damaging. Think about the language you use. Do your words open up possibilities or do they shut them down?

Experiment [1]

I am going to ask you two questions, but you don't have to actually answer them. I want you to notice your physiological response; that is, how your body feels when you consider each question. If you are with other people, ask them to observe any shifts in you as well. Ready to play?

Question #1

What is the *worst* thing about your life right now?

Simply note your observations:

_____

Okay now, here is Question # 2

What is the *best* thing about your life right now?

Your observations: _____

I imagine you had very different physiological responses to the two questions.

Note that I changed only **one** word in those questions. I changed the word from "worst" to "best." Notice how one word can make a difference. That is the power of language.

SHIFTING TO GENERATIVE LANGUAGE

Use language that keeps the brain in a toward state and moves you toward possibilities rather than away from a problem.

To help achieve our overtone we want to make the shift to using language that creates forward motion. Neuroscience says that to generate creativity and insight we want to keep the mind moving toward possibilities rather than away from a problem. Generative language keeps the brain in that toward state while non-generative language keeps us stuck right where we are, and can even take us backward.

Generative Language Opens Possibilities

Generative Language can open up space for new, different, changed or expanded possibilities. Instead of using constrictive words that imply absolutes (and therefore shut down possibilities) such as *never, always* or *forever,* shift to generative language that opens possibilities with words or phrases such as *sometimes, in some situations, I have had experiences when..., In the past I..., I have found..., It is possible that...*

Generative Language Creates Choice

Our use of obligation language, such as *I have to, I should, you must, I'm supposed to,* implies a lack of choice and is restrictive.

Shift to generative language that infers choice, internal commitment, and other possibilities. After you do, watch the energy and conversation change almost immediately.

Shift to words such as *I would like to, I could, I want, I allow, I get to.*

Think about how you will feel when you approach your dreaded lengthy "Must Do" list by instead describing it as your "Get to Do"[2] list.

Generative Language Keeps the Scene Going

In improvisational theatre (improv), a basic principle is to *keep the scene going*. In other words, no matter how outrageous the setting or incident, or regardless of what wacky idea your partner throws at you, you must take the scene and run with it without blocking the action. Your goal in improv is to build on what your partner says and to have the scene succeed. If you shut your partner's idea down, the scene is effectively over.

"But is an argument for our limitations."
— Anonymous

Think about the language you use in your daily life. Instead of the "Yes, but" habit switch to "Yes, and." Keep your language generative by building on an idea and adding to it. *YES* really is the most positive word in the English language.

In the 2008 Movie *Yes Man*, actor Jim Carrey plays a character whose life is at a standstill. He goes to a lecture by a self-help guru author and makes a covenant to say Yes to every opportunity that presents itself for one year. Though it is a typical Hollywood movie and the charismatic Carrey takes it over the top, *Yes Man* does make a point about the power of language. Once Carrey opened himself to saying yes, his life started to transform.

Don't Say Don't

Much as the word *yes* opens up possibilities, one other oft-used word does the opposite. I classify *don't* as one of the worst four letter words in the English language. In fact, that one word can insidiously work against your desired state.

When we precede a statement with *don't*, the brain only registers the words that follow it and therefore goes to the very place that you do *not* want to go!

- If I say, "Don't think about the pink elephant in the middle of the room," your mind instantly visualizes a pink elephant in the middle of the room.

- If I say, "Honey, don't forget your keys…" the possibility that you might "forget" is now in your head.
- If in a chorus rehearsal your director says, "Don't lose pitch", the words "lose pitch" are now reinforced.

How often does that four-letter word creep into our language – both when used with others and when used in our self-talk? To open possibilities and get unstuck, Flip It! (Chapter 3) and ask for what you want, instead of what you don't want.

Think about how you talk to yourself. Is your self-talk generative? We will get further into this in our self-talk chapter (Chapter 14). For the moment, stay with awareness and begin to notice the language you tend to use in the different parts of your life. Do you generally use language that focuses on what is not working or on what is wrong? If you do, you are miring yourself in scarcity and will stay stuck until you 'Flip it.'

We can apply generative thinking and language to all parts of our lives, teams, and organizations. Most important for those in leadership positions is to model this way of working and talking in both conversation and written communication.

Quick Guide – Words to Switch

Instead of:	Use:
I'll try	I will
I have to	I could , I want to, I get to
I should	I could
I must	I could, I would like to, I want to
Don't	Do
But	And
You must, You should	Think about, Consider
Try this	Do this
Problems	Challenges, Opportunities
Never, Always, Forever	Sometimes, In some situations, I have had experiences when, I have found…, It is possible that…

SECTION THREE
Building the Overtone Foundation

Think of the process of building your overtone foundation as if you are constructing a skyscraper. If you want to build a life, a team, or a business that fulfills its highest potential and goes beyond the sum of its parts to create an overtone, you have to build it on a strong foundation.

This chapter will outline the key building blocks of a solid, unshakeable foundation upon which you, your family, your work teams, and organizations can create overtones.

Warning!

My experience in working through this process with groups is that there is often an itch, especially by the leadership, to move along at a pace that might not allow for total buy-in of all members. The desire to jump past some of the foundational pieces and go straight into strategies and actions is a trap that will lead to short-term gain for long-term pain.

The process of inclusion does take longer and it's not necessarily a straight line from A to B. For some leaders, the process of involving others may seem like a make-work project. Remember that leading is not about you; it is about the people you lead. If you are moving too quickly, skipping steps for expediency, you will be leaving people behind and weakening your organizational structures.

Using the building analogy, it would be like adding the concrete before the rebar is in place. You and your organization will benefit from taking the time to think through the foundational pieces in this chapter methodically. Get input and buy-in from your team, and you'll move strategically toward alignment.

In keeping with the generative and growth mindset approach we adopted in the Overtone Approach section of this book, think of these building blocks as an ever-growing, expanding framework upon which your overtone will be built, not as a fixed, immovable slab of concrete.

This is a *living* foundation and must be revisited on a regular basis to keep it alive and relevant.

Chapter 6
THE CRITICAL VALUE OF VALUES

*"Core values go beyond our behaviors and our wants. Without being
intentional about our values, we live backwards. We often let our
behaviors define our values. Values should define our behaviors."* [1]
— John G. Blumberg, Author

The most important building block of your overtone foundation is
the definition of your values. Your values are deeply-held views of
what you find most important at a core level. Values, both consciously and unconsciously, act as guides and drivers for your life.

The word *value* comes from the Old French verb (13c.) *valoir*, meaning:
be worth. Doing the work to clearly identify and bring your core values
to life will create a strong foundation upon which to serve the world in a
meaningful and impactful way. When you then align your values with your
behaviors and goals you spark energy at a deep level that will motivate and
inspire your overtone.

Values as Your Foundation

Your values provide an unfaltering foundation of strength as you wend your
way through the complexities of life. Besides acting as the foundational
blocks of your personal life, values also form critical operating principles in
a company or organization. In addition, values that are strongly defined and
actively lived can help organizations withstand adversity and amplify success.
Those who have either not yet defined their important operating values or
those who have written out their values and merely shoved them in a drawer,
are doing themselves and their organizations a disservice.

There is a distinction between the values that we profess to believe in – and our "values in action" – those values which guide our behavior. It is not enough to simply state what you believe in. In order to create a strong foundation you must align values with behaviors, and actively and consistently bring them to life.

Values as Drivers and Influencers

Your values influence and drive the ways in which you live and work (either consciously or unconsciously). The activities you undertake, how you lead, the policies you make, how you act, and how you walk through this world are all driven by values. Values influence your direction, plans, and focus. For instance, if *equality* is one of your top values, how might that influence your work as a lawyer? Imagine how many in the service professions hold *caring* or *compassion* as top core values. This is no accident.

Doing this values work in any member-based organization is a vital way to begin to find your organization's overtone. A critical part of this process is to be fully inclusive and give an opportunity for every person to participate and give input.

Values as Guides

One of my competitive choral group clients was creating a new vocal qualification program for members, with the goal of raising musical standards. This was a source of endless circular discussion amongst the musical leadership. By reflecting back to the chorus's core value statement, which was "respect and support for continuous growth of the individual," the leadership team was able to craft an inclusive and celebratory program rather than a judgmental, "testing" one. The revised focus made the program an educational growth experience for members and was widely embraced. The stated group values acted as a touchstone to guide their planning.

Your personal or company values can act as a guide for any operational or strategic discussion. Clear values can save time by simplifying decision-making. Strongly defined values that have been created by, and agreed to, by members, can also be used as guides for difficult conversations in the event that one of the members gets off-track. (See Chapter 18 *Bitsy Fairhaven.*) By framing a critical conversation in the context of a desire to uphold agreed-upon values, you can provide perspective and shift focus away from the personal.

Values as Course Correctors and Decision Makers

Marilyn is CFO of a multi-million dollar company that sells consumer products. She was extremely upset at sales department personnel who were routinely abusing their expense accounts and running up massive bills entertaining clients and partying amongst themselves. The sales team brushed off her inquiries into their expenses and though her CEO also dismissed her concerns, he continued to pester her about the company's bottom line. She felt responsible for the financial health of the company, yet could neither effect change nor get any support for her plea to keep the partying to a reasonable level.

Marilyn was hugely stressed, with a big knot in her stomach every Sunday night as she thought about returning to work the next day. Upon exploration, she realized that her strong personal values of honesty, transparency, equality, and fiscal responsibility were not aligned with the company operating culture. (The company had not yet created operational values.) She realized how critical it was for her to find a workplace that respected and supported her strong values, and that alignment was hugely important for her state of mind and overall well-being. She made the decision to seek other employment and is now flourishing in a new company.

When we live or work out of alignment with our values, we can feel off-kilter, uneasy, or even unwell. A company out of alignment with its values will not be as successful, nor will its employees be engaged to their full potential. Working for a company or a boss who does not honor your values can create an irreconcilable crisis.

Most of us will, at one time or another, have found ourselves in situations that just don't feel good in our hearts and guts. In these instances, we may well have been in situations where our values weren't present or upheld. If we are in tune with our values, the message we receive from situations such as this can act as a catalyst for course correction.

Values as Support

Living in alignment with one's deepest core values can provide much needed support when the road gets rocky. Values alignment is the soothing honey elixir that allows one to sleep after disastrous crises of faith.

REFLECTION OPPORTUNITY

1. What are the values you personally hold as most important?

2. How do those values show up in your life or influence your behaviors?

3. How do the values you hold as important change in different parts of your life?

4. What are your corporate or organizational values?

5. How do your corporate values drive your business?

6. How do you keep those values present?

* *The Overtone Effect Workbook* has detailed worksheets to help you work through your values identification and reflection comprehensively. See back page.

Chapter 7
GUIDING PRINCIPLES

Now that you have established your core values, your next step is to drill down and identify what those values mean – in practice. How do you live your values? It is all well and good to hold a value of, for example, *integrity*, but what does living in "integrity" mean in real terms? In other words, how will you know you are upholding that value?

Creation of guiding principles will form a manifesto for how to live your life or conduct your business. They are brief statements that will inform the cultural practices of your life or organization. They bring your values to life in an active way, with a clear connection between the values you hold and how you commit to evidencing them as behaviors. Putting your values to work in concrete terms will add clarity and direction to every aspect of your life.

On a personal level your guiding principles articulate your deepest commitment to the way you want to live. Using the value of integrity, as an example, a guiding principle could be, "I say what I mean and mean what I say."

For an organization, understanding what your values mean in terms of behavior is critical. For example, a value of *commitment* could mean different things to different people. When you understand and agree collectively on a guiding principle that says perhaps "we are all committed to do our personal best," an understanding of what that value means is clear. These guiding principles can inform everything from HR practices to strategic planning. If there is a disconnect between the guiding principles and company values then you will be hard-pressed to feel the Overtone Effect.

REFLECTION OPPORTUNITY

<u>Guiding Principles</u>

Think about your values and how they could form statements to act as guiding principles. Take one of your values and create three statements that have meaning for you in how they evidence themselves in behaviors.

<u>Groups</u>: Get full input around the meaning of your group's values. Be sure to create a safe forum that allows everyone to express freely their meaning of the values your group is living. Use the discussion as a learning entry point to come to consensus on your manifesto.

Chapter 8
MAXIMIZING STRENGTHS

"People have several times more potential for growth when they invest energy in developing their strengths instead of correcting their deficiencies." [1]
—Tom Rath, *StrengthsFinder 2.0*

O ur intrinsic qualities and strengths form fundamental building blocks of our overtone foundation. By recognizing, acknowledging, and working from our strengths, we can become the best we can possibly be. Identifying and maximizing our strengths are critical steps in moving us forward personally, as well as with teams and organizations. Living into our strengths brings us alignment, happiness, and joy, and helps us create our overtone.

Oddly, our society has led us to believe that instead of building on strengths, we are better off to place our focus on correcting our deficiencies. Our school system is built on that premise. Little Stevie brings home a report card with an A in English and a D in Math, so the energy and focus for the next term is on bringing his math marks up. I am not saying that math is not important, but what might happen for Stevie if focus and attention were also paid to his skill in English? How could amplifying that strength serve Stevie – not only in adding skill levels but also in giving him self-worth and confidence?

Under the twenty-five year leadership of Sandy Marron, Championship Master 700 musical director, the Vancouver-based Lions Gate Chorus[2] has risen in the International Chorus competitions from 22nd (out of 28 choruses) in 1996 to 3rd place in 2007. Ever since then, the chorus has maintained Top Five placements. Sandy has an ambitious vision and strives for a high standard of musical excellence. A self-proclaimed musical geek, she has a natural inclination to work the details of every phrase to perfection. She learned the hard way that sometimes spending too long trying to fix something can be counter-productive. It can serve to batter down the singers, reduce their confidence, and shut down the environment for learning.

Sandy hasn't stopped her focus on excellence in any way. She sees the strengths in her singers and acknowledges them so that the chorus members are open to receive and learn. This acknowledgment produces confidence and fuels their desire to perform better. She puts them in the generative growth mindset that is so critical. It was a revelation for Sandy to discover that she didn't have to lower her musical standards, and that by working from strengths she can achieve more than focusing solely on correcting the weaknesses.

The work in the area of Strengths-based Psychology, founded by Dr. Donald O. Clifton, supports this generative approach. Clifton worked with author Tom Rath and a team of Gallup scientists with "a goal of starting a global conversation about what's right with people."[3] They created the online StrengthsFinder assessment tool that has helped millions worldwide to discover and develop their natural talents.

Taking a generative approach and working from a foundation of strengths can amplify what is already good and turn it into great. What could feel better than knowing that our biggest successes will come from magnifying our innate talents and abilities?

Success is the art of being who we already are.

Interestingly, I have found three consistent holdbacks in people of all ages in different areas of the world: 1) an inability to recognize; 2) a tendency to downplay; and 3) a reluctance to acknowledge their own unique gifts. These holdbacks are by far the most persistent barriers to living into their personal overtones. Sometimes people don't recognize their strengths or acknowledge them as special because they are the intuitive, easy things that they can do without thinking. In fact, those strengths and qualities you exhibit unconsciously are often your signature strengths; that is, the ones that set you apart from others.

There seems to be universal discomfort with identifying and stepping into one's own strengths, and it stems from many factors. Some of those factors may be cultural, or a result of parental or societal influences, or they may be derived from personal experience.

Certainly in much of North America, many of us were brought up to believe that modesty is a virtue and that promoting or celebrating our gifts is considered boastful. We Canadians are known for being self-effacing, retiring, modest, and even apologetic. In fact, when asked to identify their core strengths, my workshop participants are often uncomfortable and literally start to squirm in their seats.

While in Minnesota I discovered a cultural phenomenon known as "Minnesota Nice." According to Wikipedia, this phenomenon manifests itself in characteristics that include "polite friendliness, a tendency toward understatement, a disinclination to stand out, emotional restraint, and self-deprecation." (Traits typical of this stereotype are also generally applied to neighboring Canadians.)

My Minnesotan friends freely acknowledged these characteristics, and I kept that in mind as I worked with high-level singers there. We consciously worked to leave "Minnesota Nice" behind, and explored how intentionally celebrating their signature brilliance and consistently acknowledging strengths could build their confidence, and grow their performance potential.

In Scandinavian countries there is a set of cultural rules called the Law of Jante, which are expressions of variations on the general theme of "don't think you are anyone special." Imagine how that theme could adversely affect a world-renowned Swedish chorus as they prepare for an international a cappella singing competition.

Britt-Heléne Bonnedahl, co-director of Sweden's Rönninge Show Chorus[4] (the 2017 and 2014 World a cappella chorus champions), understands this conundrum all too well. She knows that in order for Rönninge to grow into its potential as an ensemble she must help build the belief in each singer that she is indeed special.

To help with that, she promotes a positive philosophy and incorporates extensive mental training. Members are first encouraged to identify their limiting beliefs, then burn and reframe them to change them into a desired picture of the self and the singer they want to be. They then live into that picture as if it is happening now. Britt-Heléne actively encourages a generative environment of looking at and listening to what is right, rather than what is wrong.

I encourage you all to consider blowing your cultural and social patterns out the window. Instead, bring your brilliance to the forefront and step into it fully. Think of the possibilities!

"What, you say? I have no brilliance. I am only average." Let's get one thing straight – everyone in this world is unique. In fact, your DNA and your particular set of life experiences have created a *You* who is different from anyone else. Those differences, the unique *You*, is your signature brilliance. Your greatest contribution to the world will be realized when you figure out what your distinctive brilliance is and live into that. For the greatest and easiest path to success, you simply need to be more of who you already are. Focus your energies on increasing your capacity in those areas in which you have natural ability. Be more *You*.

> *"Today you are you! That is truer than true! There is no one alive who is you-er than you!"* [5]
> —Dr. Seuss

Not convinced? Consider this: it is selfish *not* to acknowledge your strengths and step into them. By embracing your strengths, you will be more of the best parts of you, and the whole world benefits. Playing small shuts down the possibilities of finding your overtone or contributing fully to the creation of one for your organization.

When I work with groups and teams, I encourage each member to consider that their greatest contribution to the team will be when they show up fully as themselves. The different aspects of every individual in a collective are what make the group unique. Celebrating, valuing, and encouraging the expression of the differences of each member is the key to a group's growth and success.

Imagine a world in which everyone was encouraged to live from and explore his or her greatest capacity. Spend some time today appreciating and encouraging your colleagues, your partner, and your children's strengths and talents. Watch how they grow!

Identifying Strengths

First, and most importantly, you must do the work of identifying your strengths. A strengths-based approach to work and life has been proven to develop individuals at a far greater rate than an approach focused on correcting deficiencies. What are the qualities that you possess that contribute the most to this world? What makes you *you*?

What strengths does your organization already have? What strengths form the foundation of its overtone? If that's a tough one for your organization to answer, this could well be the biggest area of potential improvement – the "growing edge" area – to focus on for maximum impact.

REFLECTION OPPORTUNITY

Creating your I AM list

Grab a piece of paper and set the timer for three minutes. The reason for the short time allotment is so that you are not tempted to over think this exercise and start justifying your responses.

Write a list of all of your qualities and strengths. Dig deep and get at the strength underneath a learned skill. For example, instead of saying you are a good accountant, write the qualities you have that make you a good accountant such as being analytical or thorough. Aim to create a list of twenty. Okay, start the timer!

How did you do? If you got stuck, ask those close to you what they see in you. Ask your friends why they like to hang around with you, ask your spouse why he or she married you, etc.

Overtone Tip: Keep your I AM list handy and read it daily

Stepping Into Strengths

Once you have acknowledged your strengths, think about how you can really step into them. How could you show up as more Jan, more Jeff, more Dianne? How could you be the most of the best parts of yourself most often? Focus your energies on increasing your capacity in those areas in which you have natural ability. Be more You. Consciously think about ways to align your life and your goals with your natural talents.

> Gallup studies indicate that, *"People who do have the opportunity to focus on their strengths every day are six times as likely to be engaged in their jobs and more than three times as likely to report having an excellent quality of life in general."* [6]
> —Tom Rath, *StrengthsFinder 2.0*

REFLECTION OPPORTUNITY

Top Strengths Identification

Which of the strengths on your I AM list are the ones you most often employ or are ones that stand out for you as your "go-to" strengths?

For this exercise, simply rank your top three strengths.

Note that your "go-to" strengths may change for certain environments or with different relationships, so go ahead and create different categories for work, home, etc. if you like.

Optimizing Your Strengths

I am a certified facilitator for the Strength Deployment Inventory® (SDI®), the critical tool in Relationship Awareness Theory®[7] developed forty years ago by Dr. Elias Porter. The useful thing about this tool (unlike many other assessments I have encountered in my career) is that it goes deeper than a surface description of your personality or style. The SDI gets at your

Motivational Values underneath your behavior so as to illuminate what uniquely drives you, both in good times and in times of conflict. The application of the SDI to relationships and team interaction is huge. Imagine if you actually understood what motivated someone! Think of the ways you might then be able to shift your behavior to relate to that person more successfully.

One of the four tenets of the SDI is that a weakness is simply an overdone or misapplied strength (either actually overdone, or overdone through the filter of someone else's lens.) In order to have the greatest possible success in engaging, relating to, and communicating with others, we must access and maximize a balanced blend of our signature strengths. When we get attached to, or over-rely on, the use of a particular strength, relationship misunderstandings or breakdowns in communication occur. That interferes with accessing our overtone.

Are you sometimes too much of a good thing? What would the top ranked strengths on your I AM list look like if overdone? For example, I decided my go-to strength was self-confidence. However, self-confidence, if overdone, could come across as intimidating, controlling, arrogant, or even manipulative! Even though my intent is positive as I use my self-confidence strength, the effect on others may be something quite different (and unintended.)

To optimize your strengths, think about which of your less-used strengths you could use in each situation to balance and enhance your go-to strengths. That way, they will be are perceived in the way you intend and will enhance your communication.

For example, let's say I am running a staff meeting and I identify "self-confidence" as my go-to strength. Armed with the knowledge that self-confidence (if overdone or perceived as being so) could be intimidating to some of my staff, I could augment my self-confidence by borrowing other strengths of mine that wouldn't ordinarily be as present in that situation – such as flexibility or caring. My more rounded-out presence would create a better atmosphere for successful communication during that meeting.

Drawing on and utilizing all of your I AM strengths can add much-needed depth and dimension to your personality and enhance your effectiveness.

REFLECTION OPPORTUNITY

Strengths Overdone

1. What might your top ranked strengths look like if they were overdone or overdone through the filter of someone else's lens?
2. Think of some situations where you might borrow one of your less-used strengths to good result to ameliorate one of your potentially overdone top strengths.

Chapter 9
VISION: THINKING OUTSIDE THE DOT

There's an old story of two stonecutters who were asked what they were doing. The first said, "I'm cutting this stone into blocks." The second replied, "I'm on a team that's building a cathedral."

A re you cutting stone into blocks, or do you, like the cathedral builder, have a bigger vision – one that inspires your life and work? A vision is a vivid articulation of a desired future and answers the question, "What are you building?" Clarifying what is important to you and creating an evocative picture of your future is a key component of your overtone journey. Without a vision, your journey will be directionless.

"It's not what the vision is; it's what the vision does." [1]
-Robert Fritz, *The Path of Least Resistance*

A vision will add energy and excitement, and garner support for your journey and life legacy. Martin Luther King said, "I have a dream", not "I have a plan." His dream galvanized a nation. Some of my clients are afraid to dream and give voice to that which seems impossible in the present moment. My question to them is: "What's the downside?" A vision will add energy to your strategic planning. A vision is a beacon of light to keep you heading in the right direction. We have the choice of either living a default future (one where we simply react to events), or a creative future (one that we proactively create and live into based on our dreams.) Which will you choose?

Connecting with your vision and aligning with your values will guide you on your journey to find your overtone. Back to the analogy of building a skyscraper – one must envision how high the building will be, and what it could look like, before beginning to lay the foundation.

The Impossible is Possible

Does your vision seem out of reach? All through history ordinary folk like you and me have achieved the impossible. Boundaries have been constantly stretched and unthinkable dreams have become everyday norms. People have done things that no one, not even they, thought possible.

In 1961, U.S. President John F Kennedy announced his bold goal of putting a man on the moon before the end of the 60s. Though JFK was not alive to witness it, Neil Armstrong made his famous moonwalk in 1969.

Women didn't even have the right to vote in Canada's federal elections until 1918, but Agnes Macphail dreamed of representing her farming community and making change. In 1921, she became Canada's first female Member of Parliament, the only woman out of 235 MPs. (Note: In 2015 women were elected in 88 out of 338 seats)

No one thought it possible to transplant a heart into another human, and yet Dr. Christiaan Barnard did just that in 1967. Now, over four thousand heart transplants are done every year.

Athletic feats once deemed impossible are now a matter of course. In 1954, Roger Bannister shattered records and ran the four-minute mile. At the time, no one thought that was possible, yet now the four-minute mile is considered standard for a middle-distance athlete. In 1980, Canadian hero Terry Fox, after losing a leg to cancer, had a dream of running across Canada and raising one dollar from every Canadian, which would have been $24 million at that time. He ran the equivalent of a full marathon on one leg every day. Sadly, his run was cut short by a return of cancer, but since then over $650 million has been raised in his name in community runs around the world.

Each of these people had a vision, and a belief in the possibility of achieving their dream.

I am sure there has been a time in your life that you did something you never dreamed or thought possible. Perhaps you are doing something now that twenty years ago would have seemed out of the question.

Our human capacity is infinite. All we need is a dream, a willingness to break our own glass ceiling, and a commitment to our greatest success.

REFLECTION OPPORTUNITY

Tuning in to Possibility

1. When in your life have you done something that you never could have imagined you would do?
2. How do you feel now having done that unimaginable thing?

Creating your Vision

When you look at the preceding page what do you see?

Most people see a black dot in the center of the page. That black dot represents the *now* – everything that is currently present in your life, which includes your work, your leisure activities, your friends, your relationships, your home, etc. Naturally, most of us spend our time, our energy, and our thoughts in the black dot. We are moms, employees, bosses; we have dogs and apartments; we have chorus rehearsals and presentations for work. That's who we are and that's what's happening right now.

You will notice that the black dot is very small compared to the rest of the page. The black dot represents what *is* right now and the beautiful expansive white space around that dot holds the possibilities for your life.

It is time for us to think outside the dot. Put your mind into that glorious white space of possibilities and the potential of what could be. If anything is possible – without limitation – what do you see? Look deep inside, at what is yearning to be expressed.

"Your vision will become clear only when you can look into your own heart. Who looks outside, dreams; who looks inside, awakes." [2]
—Carl Jung

Grab a big piece of paper, put a dot in the center and allow yourself to dream of your possibilities. Jot down images, words, phrases, feelings, things, and activities in the white space around the dot. Dream without limits. Bring your vision to life. Often the first thoughts you have are the most important ones so let your inner critic/judge go. Stop second-guessing yourself. If *any-thing* is possible, what might be there?

James was knee-deep in an overhaul of his business. He came to me wanting some coaching around the rebranding of his company. If I had jumped in and coached him around the specifics of what that rebrand would mean for him, we probably would have got caught up in the details of practical matters like his website redesign. Instead, I encouraged him to draw back the lens and paint me a picture of his business six months down the road. "What would be there?" I then drew the lens out further – to ten years down the road. It was then that the energy shifted in his tone, and you could feel the passion in his voice as he described a vision he had never stated aloud. James had a dream of going town to town in a developing country providing leadership coaching to youth. Articulation of this vision added compelling fuel to the direction of his business.

This visioning work is pivotal in understanding what is important to you, or to your organization. If you are part of a team or community group be sure to involve everyone. Build your big, bold vision together. Keep expanding beyond what might seem possible right now. Keep away from the how-to-do thoughts. Strategizing can come later.

After doing the *Thinking Outside the Dot* exercise and seeing everything she imagined in her bright possible future, one of my clients said, "Wow, looking at that makes me tired." My challenge to her was to go back, look at her pictures and, instead of thinking of the process to get there, to place herself in that vision in the present tense. Next, I asked her to do a personal check-in about how each of the pictures in her vision energized her. If they still felt tiring, then it was possible she had included something she thought she *should* put there that wasn't really coming from her. Perhaps it was something that wasn't intimately aligned and connected with her values and foundation. This same check-in can be done with your group on a regular basis to make sure the vision is still inspiring and energizing.

What's next?

> *A vision without action is a daydream*
> *Action without vision is a nightmare*
> —Japanese Proverb

The Japanese proverb says it simply and clearly. Once you have established your vision, you have to take *action* to live into the vision – it doesn't just happen. You may have read some law of attraction writings that seem to indicate that if you simply visualize a red Ferrari in your driveway, one day it will be there. In actual fact, wishing won't make it happen – you must take action. However, if you do put that thought and picture of a red Ferrari in your driveway in your brain, your mind will then get working on how best to take action to make that dream a reality.

From the coaching work I have done, it seems that most people understand the concept of making strategies and developing tactical action plans to achieve a particular result. There's not much to be gained from a general discussion of these, as they will differ in each case. Just be certain to connect your strategies and actions to your compelling vision. If you base your actions on your values, you will begin to create your overtone.

"A vision has the impelling force of a long line of music ... It invites infinite expression, development, and proliferation within its definitional framework." [3]
—Rosamund Stone Zander and Benjamin Zander,
The Art of Possibility

The journey to living into our vision is rarely a straight path, nor is there one way to reach that shimmering picture. A vision is something you work toward, a changing picture – not a fixed place where you arrive. It is always evolving, shifting and growing – that's what makes it vibrant and compelling. Be open to flexing and revisiting it. Changing worlds, lives, personnel, and business climates could mean that your vision will naturally also need to change.

Be sure to acknowledge and celebrate each signpost reached along the way. If you hold off on celebrating your triumphs until some elusive end is reached, you cheat yourself of the joy of the journey.

Reconnect and be inspired on a daily basis by your vision, supported by your values, qualities, and strengths. When we acknowledge our sense of value in the world and contribute and connect to others, we share naturally and receive continually.

REFLECTION OPPORTUNITY

<u>Thinking Outside the Dot</u>

Imagine living your *Thinking Outside the Dot* possibilities:
   1. What could that mean for you and those around you?
   2. How would you feel?
   3. What might change for you?
Now that you've established it, how will you stay connected to your vision?

Chapter 10
WHAT IS YOUR WHY?

You have now identified your values – the fundamental guides and influencers for your life – and you have created a compelling vision that connects and aligns with those values. You have acknowledged who you are, the strengths you bring to the world, and you have a clear idea of the core operating principles for your life or business. That work creates an unshakeable foundation upon which to build your overtone. Excellent!

It is time for me to ask you a provocative question: What is your WHY? What do you stand for? What is the Why that really drives your vision?

Often called "mission" or "purpose," the Why question, once answered, will complete the foundational trifecta that we started with values and vision.

In Simon Sinek's popular TED talk and book, *Start with Why*[1], he examined how we must always start with Why, before going to the What and How. Why is our reason, our cause, and will add juice to our vision and strategies.

We live our lives day to day caught up in the "hows" without remembering or considering our Why. As a result, we are affected and thrown off course easily by external influences in our world. As soon as you understand your Why at a deep core level you will have the inner driver to inspire you. Many of us don't think about this often.

It might seem obvious that those who join a Sweet Adeline chorus do so in order to sing. But what is it really about? What is the Why? I experimented with the Lions Gate Chorus and said – "Okay, obviously we are part of a singing organization because we want to sing – but why this group? Why this chorus?" The Why that was the *real* driver for the members overwhelmingly came out as Joy. Spreading joy. Bringing joy. Feeling joy.

Your Why is the emotional element that expertly transfers the picture of your vision into your brain's memory cells. What does it feel like in your heart, your gut, and your soul when you think of your mission or purpose? Allow your body to respond to the feelings associated with the picture you have created. A compelling purpose will act as an energizer and create the momentum to inspire both you and those around you.

Creating a personal overtone is an amazing accomplishment. Imagine the possibilities when you then go beyond self to contribute your overtone to join with others. By connecting your Why purpose to others you begin to move into what might be your ultimate contribution to this world — your legacy.

REFLECTION OPPORTUNITY

What is your Why?

Step 1: If considering the Why of your entire vision feels too big, experiment with a smaller piece. Ask yourself, "Why do I do what I do?" To feel how this works, focus on your life activities and do some 'why reflection' around them.

For example, "Why are you a runner?" You might respond, "To keep fit." If you dig deeper, your Why might be something like "I always feel great after a run, my body feels strong and that fills me with confidence." Or - "Why are you in a book club?" You might answer, "I like reading." If you dig deeper and think about your Why it might be something more like, "Reading opens my mind and transports me to another place – and that feels freeing."

What happens when you dig down to your Why?

Step 2: Now look at your *Thinking outside the Dot* vision and think about the emotional, juicy passions underneath your vision.

Why is all that important? How does that connect with others? You jotted down some words in last chapter's reflections around how you would feel living those possibilities. Is your Why in there perhaps?

Chapter 11
CREATING YOUR GPS
(GUIDING PURPOSE SLOGAN)

C ould you distill the essence of your Why message to a bumper
sticker length? Though not as popular now as they were in the 70s,
the pithy statements that fit on a sticker and are affixed to one's car
bumper are captivating and memorable. We want to create that same kind of
memorable slogan to capture the crux of our Why and act like a GPS. Our
GPS (Guiding Purpose Slogan) will constantly inspire us as we work to find
our overtone.

Our GPS must stretch, energize, and move us to an ideal state or a provocative place of being. Most often our mission or purpose statement is long and unwieldy, and is buried on our website or in our company's annual report. A short GPS has the power of staying present in everything we do.

I struggled for a few years with creation of a mission/purpose statement for my coaching business. Although I finally drilled it down to one longish sentence, I could never remember the exact words when asked to repeat it. That was a big clue that it was filled with coach-speak jargon. When I finally landed on my guiding purpose slogan – my GPS – it flew off my lips and I smiled at its simplicity. ***Changing lives for the better every day***. Simple, energizing, memorable. That drives me from the time I get up and guides everything I do from the way I talk to the Starbucks barista to the way I approach my coaching work.

One of my government clients came up with a GPS for his department in order to inspire excellence at every stage of production. The Minister was the last stop – i.e. the big boss – for their work. Their GPS became ***Everything is Minister Ready***. That statement meant living into a high level of excellence and accuracy. My client took it to his department and they expanded it to apply not only in a literal sense to the accuracy of their reports, but also to the level of excellence with which they approach all of their work and relations. This GPS influenced them all in an easy-to-remember way.

The creation and repetition of a powerful and memorable energizing slogan that implies a positive outcome is a proven way to successfully inspire and guide a team.

After Canadian athletes failed to obtain a single gold medal in either the 1976 Summer Olympics hosted in Montreal, or the 1988 Winter Olympics hosted in Calgary, the Canadian Olympic Committee (COC) created a long-term commitment. Their goal was for Canada to be the top medal-winning nation in 2010, when the Winter Olympics came to Vancouver, BC. To that end, the COC started the ***Own the Podium*** program, and the Canadian government invested $120 million in training. In 2010, Canada finished with an amazing fourteen gold medals and twenty-six medals in total! Although the program did not achieve its stated goal of winning the most medals, Canada did succeed in breaking the record for most gold medals won in *any* Winter Olympics. That GPS of ***Own the Podium*** provided a provocative and expansive stimulator that inspired training programs, athletes, and the energy of the nation.

It's all happening perfectly was the GPS that inspired the Rönninge Show Chorus to achieve greatness at the International a cappella chorus competition in Honolulu, Hawaii. They became the first women's barber-shop chorus in Sweet Adelines International outside of North America to win the gold medal as well as the Audience Choice Award and the Celebrity Choice Award. It *did* all happen perfectly!

Your GPS could be a three to eight-word phrase, or as simple as a single word to galvanize the troops, like the story of the membership warehouse giant who adopted the GPS of the word *Synergy* to inspire its actions after a merger.

One couple I know created a GPS for their relationship that was three words: *Love, Respect, Joy.*

You can create a GPS for your life, your organization, your relationship, or even a specific team project. Let that slogan infuse you with purpose and passion.

Other examples of Guiding Purpose Slogans:

I have a dream - Martin Luther King

We must be the change that we envision - Mahatma Gandhi

Students First - Elsie Roy Elementary School

Yes, We can! - Barack Obama Presidential Campaign

Always Compete - Pete Carroll, Seattle Seahawks Coach

Unrelentingly Friendly Service – Reckless Bike Store

REFLECTION OPPORTUNITY

Creating Your GPS

Work from your Why and boil down the essence of your Why to a maximum eight-word slogan that could fit on a bumper sticker. Be sure that the slogan is provocative, evocative, and has some energy that moves you. Write your slogan out on a bumper sticker-sized piece of paper and put it on your wall. Do you get excited looking at it?

SECTION FOUR
Creating Your Personal Overtone

"Personal mastery is not a simplistic process of merely affirm-
ing our strengths while ignoring our weaknesses. It is, as Carl
Jung would explain it, "growth toward wholeness."… It is
about honestly facing and reconciling all facets of self." [1]
—Kevin Cashman, *Leadership from the Inside Out*

N ow that you have put in place the overtone foundation, as outlined in the chapters of Section 3, you are ready to begin the journey to find your personal overtone.

Creating your personal overtone involves being willing to look at all parts of yourself with the intention of self-discovery and personal development. You must be willing to acknowledge and accept your strengths, and become aware of your growth areas (your growing edges.) When you allow yourself to be vulnerable, when you are open to not knowing, and can go past your ego, you will grow into your overtone.

It will involve looking at your mindset, body, spirit, and heart. It will also mean actively seeking to grow, learn, and live into your best self.

Sound daunting? Rest assured, we are all on this journey together. The path may not always be smooth, but the scenery is grand.

Chapter 12
PERSONAL MASTERY

*"Everybody thinks of changing humanity, but no
one thinks of changing himself."* [1]
—Leo Tolstoy

hether it's a gold medal, a blue ribbon, or a glistening trophy,
we view those at the top of their craft, no matter what their
field of expertise, with respect and awe. Those external awards
seem to signal attainment of some sort of extra-special mastery level.

In fact, all of those award-winning musicians, athletes, and executives
know that the key to success is their commitment to continuous lifetime
growth. The awards of excellence and achievement are a signpost on the road,
not the end of the road. In his book *Outliers*, author Malcolm Gladwell[2]
writes about how it takes ten thousand hours of deliberate practice to master
a skill. Like the quest for skill mastery, creating one's personal overtone is also
a journey.

*"Personal Mastery is the phrase we use for the discipline of personal
growth and learning ... It means approaching one's life as a creative
work, living life from a creative as opposed to reactive viewpoint."* [3]
-Peter Senge, *The Fifth Discipline*

Let's take a moment to consider Senge's quote. Imagine seeing life as a
creative work, one that can be shaped by each of us in a generative way as
opposed to something that is a default or pre-determined by circumstance.

Our overtone journey will encourage us to open our thinking, choose
our own paths and direction, and perhaps even begin to see with new eyes.
It is an opportunity to reframe our thinking and go beyond a fixed view of

what is possible. We can then move to an empowered and dynamic option of living and generating our future intentionally. We will approach this personal work with the concept of mastery being a practice, a discipline, and a way of life. The personal mastery practice will inform the way we do everything and how we *be* every day. Best of all, it's a practice that is entirely in our control.

There are infinite possibilities for our lives when we are inspired to keep striving to go beyond ourselves. Lest this all sounds like too much work, remember, an overtone only exists in the present moment and the key to mastery is to stay present and live each moment. The gold is in each moment of the journey, not the end point.

The International Coach Federation (ICF)[4] is the world's leading professional association for coaches with over 20,000 members in 100 countries. The highest coaching accreditation awarded by the ICF is that of MCC – Master Certified Coach. As of May 2016, there were only 65 people awarded MCC in Canada, and only 743 worldwide.

> Marjorie Busse[5] is one of those Master Certified Coaches. An instructor of the esteemed Royal Roads University executive coaching program in Victoria, she spoke to the graduating class about her journey. "I am learning every day. In fact, the more I learn the more I realize I don't know," she said. "Even my coaching skills are getting finer tuned each day. Most importantly I think I am starting to figure out who I am – this personal mastery part is really just beginning. And the more I learn, the more I feel I can contribute."

It was inspirational to hear that Marj's quest for personal mastery, even at an elite MCC level of mastery, was ongoing and continuous - that she had never stopped learning.

Personal mastery is perhaps the most important of all intangible assets to which we can dedicate ourselves. It is the route to alignment of all facets of self – body, mind, and soul, and is the path to making change. Personal mastery will help us choose the actions and achieve the results that move us toward the attainment of our personal overtone. Finding and living in our overtone will provide benefits of increased happiness, peace, purpose, and success.

For those who are feeling like the development of personal mastery is a selfish hedonistic pursuit, remember that ultimately the path of mastery is designed for the greater good. When you are living your overtone, you create the space for others to hear and experience your overtone and are then contributing most fully to others around you.

"Personal Mastery allows us to transcend our egos and move into authentic service and authentic contribution." [6]
—Kevin Cashman, *Leadership from the Inside Out*

Personal mastery encompasses much more than mastering a particular skill. The journey begins with developing self-awareness of whom and where you are right now. Awareness with acceptance and without judgment opens the possibility for change and growth. Understanding yourself allows you to relate to others more deeply. You can't create change in others until you have created change in yourself. Self-knowledge and awareness stem from honest and deep self-examination. What are your emotional vulnerabilities, your blind spots, your biases, your values, your strengths, your growing edges?

Along with awareness, you must be open to embarking on this mastery journey. Are you willing to do the work or are you, like Gavin (in Chapter 2) resistant to change?

STEPS TO TAKE ON YOUR JOURNEY TO PERSONAL MASTERY

Create your Personal Mastery Plan

Section Three outlines, from a personal perspective, the foundational elements you need to form your Personal Mastery Plan. The plan is a template for your development and learning built on the foundation of your personal values and guiding principles. Identify your strengths and build on them, and align your foundational elements.

Define Your Current Reality

Become self-aware and willing to look at yourself without judgment or labels. See your current reality clearly for it is from that place that you launch your quest for personal mastery. Knowing exactly where you are starting from is a sensible, objective way to measure where you are journeying. Every step forward is a step forward. That is what I call the power of incremental improvement.

Establish Your Vision

Create that evocative picture of what you are building and hold it present for yourself. Keep that vision of what you are building close and refer to it daily.

Embrace the Gap between Your Vision and Current Reality

Instead of seeing the gap between where you are and where you want to be as a failure, generative thinking can help you see it as an opportunity, a challenge seeking resolution, or a new vista to conquer. World thought leader Peter Senge talks about the force generated inside ourselves due to the gap between our personal vision and our current reality. He calls this force "creative tension." [7] Tension always seeks resolution, and we move toward personal mastery when we commit ourselves to relieving that tension by cultivating generative thinking. Senge recommends that we *lean* into that creative tension.

Show Up as a Learner

Open up your world and your thinking by actively showing up as a learner in everything you do. Seek knowledge. Be curious.

Add Supports

Seek feedback around blind spots from trusted and respected people, and feed forward from those invested in your success. (See Chapter 22) Listen carefully and heed what you will. Ask for help. Enroll someone to act as your accountability partner.

Share Your Knowledge

Teaching or mentoring another is a quick-start way to deepen your personal mastery skills. Allow your knowledge and experience to enrich and influence the lives of others – and feel your inner light glow as you watch the light bulbs come on for someone else.

Challenge Yourself Daily

Do one *new* thing daily to relieve your creative tension and move you toward your vision.

Surround Yourself with People who Stretch You

It is said you are the sum of the five people you spend the most time with. Who are your Top Five? Are they actively working to improve themselves, enrich the world, contribute, and learn? If not, find some people who are, and fuel your journey with renewed energy.

> "We shall not cease from exploration, and the end of all our exploring will
> be to arrive where we started and know the place for the first time." [8]
>
> —T. S. Eliot

Chapter 13
SELF-VALUE

As you have probably ascertained from the preceding chapters, to experience the Overtone Effect, one must look within. There is no external formula for purchase on the QVC shopping network. That magical balance and alignment of parts cannot be bought or sold. Like the Dalai Lama said, it all starts with you. **If you don't go within, you'll go without.**

Doing the work starts with a fundamental question around self-value, which is an honoring and respecting of self, and a commitment to meeting one's own needs. Self-value is love and acceptance of self. By valuing ourselves fully, we will show up more easily as our best self – and therefore, give more to the world.

Suzanne is exhausted. She is a brilliant, driving CEO with a lifetime of putting others before her. She told me that is how she managed to grow and sell several businesses over her lifetime, raise a thriving family, and contribute in a volunteer role to several non-profit organizations. Her exhaustion, however, is now affecting her focus and she feels less sharp at work. As Suzanne and I worked together it became clear that the biggest contributor to her exhaustion was that she never considered, established, or worked her own needs into her life mix.

It's a common challenge with my high-achieving clients, who routinely put themselves at the bottom of their 'To Do' lists. It took a lot of digging to get Suzanne to even identify what her needs were. Without thinking, she had put them aside for so long they literally had fallen off her radar. Getting enough sleep, making sure she blocked off time to incorporate physical activity into her day, taking the time to do things she loves to do – like reading and getting out in nature – were a few of the things that weren't getting attention.

Consciously adding her needs into the mix increased her resiliency, energy levels, and effectiveness. The concept is still a work-in-progress for Suzanne, and will be pivotal to helping her move into her personal overtone.

Self-care connects with self-value. If you value yourself, you will care for yourself and your needs. Wait – if you don't care for self, does that mean you don't value self? Not necessarily. It may be that you, like Suzanne, have put yourself aside for so long you have forgotten the importance of self-care. To find and live in your overtone, it is important to balance your caring for others so that it is not done at your expense. There is a reason the safety message on airplanes instructs you to put your oxygen mask on before taking care of others. If you have passed out, you can't help anyone else. By taking care of yourself first, you will be better equipped to take care of others.

I asked Lana, a coach colleague of mine, the question, "What does self-value mean to you?" She answered, "Taking care of others." Upon further questioning she said that is how she values herself – by the value she provides to others. Her sense of self-worth was wholly dependent on external forces. That is a common feeling for many over-caring individuals in the service industries – yet it is a big barrier to achieving their overtone.

Do you place a higher value on other people's needs than on your own?

My writing accountability partner, CD, asked the question of me as I tried to explain how other tasks and people took me away from my scheduled blocks of writing time. She asked, "Why are all those things more important than you doing what you have said you really want to do for yourself?" It was an excellent question that prompted some deep self-examination and conscious personal shifts that felt awkward and somewhat unfamiliar.

If you are feeling uncomfortable reading this, *good*. That means a chord has been struck for something in your personal mastery journey, and that will make a huge difference in finding your overtone.

When you think about taking care of your needs, notice what objections are coming up for you: "That sounds selfish," "I don't have enough time to take care of me," "I am here to serve others," "I feel guilty doing things for me," etc. Be aware of those objections without self-judgment.

Self-care isn't selfishness. It is the way we will be able to find and live in our life overtone and contribute the most to the world. When our needs are fully met, we will have the capacity to serve in a greater way. When you value yourself, you will take care of yourself and your needs. Remember the oxygen mask – it is impossible to take care of others fully if you don't take care of yourself first.

Use the foundational elements of values, strengths and purpose established in Section Three to empower you to stand in a self-valuing place of inner fulfillment instead of being dependent on external validation. Remind yourself that the very core of you, your "essence," is the originating point of your unique contribution. There is only one of you in this world.

Finally, make the empowered choice to shift your mindset to the concept of being here on this earth to express, not prove yourself. Feel the lightness and liberation that brings as you continue the journey to finding your overtone.

REFLECTION OPPORTUNITY

Self-Value Check-in

What are your needs? Define them clearly in each of the following four areas.
1. Physical
2. Emotional
3. Mental
4. Spiritual

When you value your needs, how do you:
1. Take care of yourself physically, emotionally, mentally, and spiritually?
2. Talk to yourself?

Energy Awareness

The first step to making any kind of change is awareness. Managing our energy inflow and outflow is a critical part of building our personal overtone capacity. Make three columns and list the people and the activities that align in each column.

Column #1 Write down everything and everyone in your life that gives you energy. (In-flow)

Column #2 Write a list of activities and relationships in your life where you both get and give energy in relatively equal proportion. (Reciprocal flow)

Column #3 Write a list of those activities and relationships where you are giving energy, without any return. (Out-flow)

Look at your three columns. What do you notice? Are you giving more energy than is flowing to you, or is there a balance? Naturally in times of crises, our out-flow will be greater, but hopefully those are short-term situations. When we are in crisis, we will want to consciously add to the in-flow – that could be by getting support, asking for help, getting more sleep, etc. Ideally, on a regular basis, we want to have a consistently balanced proportion of energy coming in and going out.

Chapter 14
SELF-TALK

"When you are playing against yourself, you never win." [1]
—Margaret Carley

How we speak to ourselves can be either an amazing aid or a crippling barrier to finding our personal overtone. We must learn to manage the destructive negative voices that stand in our way and embrace our inner voices as helpful coaches. They can support and generatively assist us to achieve holistic harmony and balance. We must replace our negative self-talk with affirming, generative language that keeps our brains in a toward state.

Professional athletes understand this explicitly and spend focused energy and effort on the psychological part of their craft to maximize their success. They understand that the mental game and their ability to maximize the power of their brains is the key to creating the Overtone Effect.

There are many ways our sneaky inner voices can wreak havoc and be a barrier to us moving forward. One of the most pervasive ways is through self-criticism and self-judgment. Man, are we hard on ourselves!

Setting and working toward high standards for ourselves is not in itself a bad thing -- however, beating up on ourselves while working toward that high standard is a bad habit. Self-judgment and self-criticism trigger our brain's "thermometer for feelings"[2] (the amygdalae) and send us to a primitive part of our brain. It creates negativity, conflict, resentment, distrust and drama. This is, quite simply, unattractive and counter-productive, and will squash your overtone opportunities.

If self-criticism and self-judgment have become your auto-response, you have created a bad habit. The good news is you can form another habit.

"You have been criticizing yourself for years, and it hasn't worked.
Try approving of yourself and see what happens." [3]
—Louise L. Hay, best-selling self-help author

As we read in Chapter 4, our brain is capable of amazing changes. Transforming negative thinking doesn't occur instantly but it is possible. Though it takes time and commitment to create a new habit, it is possible for us to make profound, changes in how we talk to ourselves.

CREATING A NEW SELF-ACCEPTANCE PARADIGM

To continue the quest to find our overtone we want to shift our paradigm from one of unproductive self-criticism to that of self-acceptance – warts and all. Well-known writer and researcher, Brené Brown[4], describes it as a journey from "What will people think?" to "I am enough." If you believe that right here, right now, wherever you are and whoever you are is enough, you will be freed from the anxious pressure of having to be something else. Then you will be able to create the space in which your overtone can exist. Take away the shoulds, the musts, the comparisons, and the focus on lack or scarcity. You *are* enough. That is the new self-acceptance paradigm that will help you achieve your overtone.

All change starts with awareness. Are you highly self-critical? Do you routinely beat yourself up? Are you consciously aware of putting yourself down to others?

See if you recognize yourself in any of the following scenarios:

Scenario: You serve a lovely dinner to friends and they say, "Wow, this chicken is divine" and you say, "Well, the sauce is actually too runny."

Scenario: You hand a report in to your boss and she starts reading it while you are sitting in her office. Before she says anything, you immediately pipe up with, "The introduction isn't very good – I should have made it more engaging."

Scenario: You demonstrate a musical warm-up exercise in front of your chorus and immediately say, "I demonstrated that horribly. Don't do it like I did."

If you are not aware of your self-flagellation, ask a friend or your partner for their observations on how you talk about yourself. Notice if they say any of the following (or variations thereof): "Well, you are a bit hard on yourself"; "You are a perfectionist"; "You don't realize how great you are"; "You do get down on yourself" or "You tend to beat yourself up for your mistakes."

Fill your Self-Acceptance Toolbox

You may require different techniques at different times to become an accepting, supportive self-talker who uses one's incredible brain capacity for moving forward instead of being held back. Use the tools and techniques below that work best for you.

Practice Thought Replacement

When the negative thought comes into your head, notice it, and before you pay attention to it and give yourself one of your usual self-put-downs, insert a positive thought into your head about the same subject that is true. For example, "The sauce is runny" thought might turn to "What wonderful conversation we have had at this dinner party." The "I screwed up the introduction to the report" thought might switch to "I really was thorough in the body of the report." Better thoughts lead to better feelings, which lead to better action.

> *"Picture your thoughts as people passing by the front of your home. Just because they're walking by doesn't mean you have to invite them in."* [5]
> —Gladys Edmunds, author and business consultant

Create Structured Obsessing Time

Sometimes you might just feel like a bit of wallowing and self-trash-talking. Okay – give yourself that, but recognize that you are making a choice and the decision to do it. Do it intentionally. Give yourself a time limit of perhaps a maximum of one hour. I call this structured obsessing time. I guarantee it will become less interesting when you force yourself to focus on it.

Do an Inventory of Past Experiences

If self-talk is leading you to self-doubt, think about where you have been successful before. Focus on those experiences and use those successes to guide your current actions.

Get Support

Enroll others close to you (or a coach!) to help you make your personal paradigm shift. Ask them to reflect back to you when they notice you putting yourself down. Ask them to help keep you on a more generative track.

Celebrate

Celebrate each time you catch yourself self-trash talking and are able to reframe your thoughts. Even a small celebration or reward releases a shot of congratulatory dopamine, which reinforces the reframed behavior.

REFLECTION OPPORTUNITY

Moving from Self-Criticism to Self-Acceptance

Create Awareness

For a full week get a notepad and jot down all of your self-critical talk. Include out-loud talk as well as the negative inner voices in your head. Ask friends what they notice and reflect on their observations. Observe when others put themselves down and how that makes you feel. On another page jot down all of the times you said something positive about yourself to others. What do you notice about this page? Was it filled or rather empty?

Analyze

Once you are aware of your negative auto thoughts, notice if there is a pattern of when that ugly monster starts talking out loud. Is it in certain areas of your life? With certain people? (Remember, this is an observation exercise, not a judgment.)

Assess the Impact

Ask yourself what those negative self-put-downs do for you. How does beating yourself up move you forward? What positive results do the self-put-downs offer?

Stay Objective

Ask yourself, "Are my thoughts true?" (E.g., from the scenario earlier: Was the sauce for the chicken too runny?) If your answer is "Yes," then rather than focusing on and expanding this one culinary failure into a sweeping condemnation like "I can't cook" or "I am a terrible host", keep objective about the matter at hand.

Practice Acceptance

Ok, the sauce is runny. Is there anything you can do about it right now? Probably not. Did the sauce ruin the dinner party? I doubt it. What could mar the joy of the party are your negative comments on the sauce, focusing on your failure and therefore making your guests feel uncomfortable because they see your distress.

Use your toolbox

Use any of the tools discussed earlier to move to self-acceptance.

LIMITING BELIEFS

The glass ceiling metaphor that describes the invisible, unbreakable barrier that keeps women and minorities from rising to the top of the corporate ladder (regardless of their qualifications or achievements) is a well-documented and sad reality. The even more insidious and crippling barriers to achieving our overtone are our self-imposed mental limitations – our own "glass ceiling."

What limits do you put on your success? What dialogue do you have with yourself that holds you back and keeps you playing small? Almost everyone has experienced first-hand the effects of limiting self-talk. Maybe it prevented you from pursuing a new job, a new adventure, or even a new relationship. Some of our limiting beliefs were taught to us, some were modeled for us by our elders, and some we learned or picked up by osmosis. Some were arrived at by as little as one simple off-hand comment from a teacher or a sibling, years earlier. We then attached importance to that comment, gave energy to it, and that limiting belief became our truth.

To conquer these limiting beliefs and break through our glass ceiling, we need to have an awareness of the barriers we put in our way and the things we do to sabotage our success. As always, awareness is the first critical step to change. Once aware, we must then be *willing* to change. We must be willing to think differently, to risk, explore, be vulnerable, and even fail in order to get different results. And thinking differently might mean simply letting go of who we think we have to be.

Marianne is a senior manager at a financial institution. She is confident, competent, and in her professional life, she has been the one in charge. She always felt she had to take a leadership role because that is who she was, and that is what people expected of her.

She could never admit to feeling less than confident and couldn't understand that she might need some support and guidance to get her through the tough times. Instead, when the tough times hit her, she felt guilty because she couldn't handle everything in the way that she usually did. Her limiting beliefs centered on the fact that she felt she couldn't be anything other than the confident, in-control leader.

Marianne's situation may perhaps be different from how we normally think about limiting beliefs, but is no less restrictive for Marianne. Her limiting beliefs stopped her from being able to step into her full self and find her personal overtone.

What limiting beliefs are barriers for you? How often do the words "I can't" pop into your head? We now know that we can rewire our thinking and our view of success. The brain can change with repeated and directed attention toward that desired change. Our human capacity is infinite. We can't be sure right now what our life possibilities are so why limit them? If living into your dreams and vision doesn't feel a bit uncomfortable, then you are probably limiting yourself and playing small. **Remember: The bigger the dream, the bigger the self-doubt.**

REFLECTION OPPORTUNITY

Personal Limiting Beliefs

1. Think of a Limiting Belief you have about yourself.
2. Where did that belief come from?
3. Truth Meter: Put your limiting belief up to scrutiny on the Truth Meter. On a scale of 1 to 10, how true is your statement? Can you be sure that your limiting belief is 100% true? Ask trusted friends what they think.
4. Embrace the Possibilities: If the truth meter shows your limiting belief as not 100% true, you have a new possibility. What might be different for you if you believed that possibility?
5. The Shift: How would your thinking need to shift to begin to move forward with this new possibility?

TURNING YOUR INNER CRITIC INTO AN INNER COACH

Living into our overtone will require us to accept ownership and control of our inner thoughts and voices that talk to us nonstop all day long. In my book, *Harmony from the Inside Out*, I described those thoughts and voices as "ducks" because they are always "quack, quack, quacking." In the heat of the moment, when the quacking gets too loud, we simply "shut the duck up."

> *"The intuitive mind is a sacred gift and the rational mind is a faithful servant. We have created a society that honors the servant and has forgotten the gift."* [6]
> —Albert Einstein

Though they may seem negative, those voices can be a sacred gift. If we reframe how we view our inner critic, and think of our inner voices as our wise self instead of our worst enemy, we can begin to shift them from critic to coach.

"How can that inner voice be my wise self?" you ask. "All it does is criticize me."

My answer is this: That criticism is all you hear, because the negative energy is powerful. However, you can take control of the situation, and with your rational mind check in with that intuitive voice and use it for good.

Professional coaches believe that every person has the answers within themselves. A coach simply asks the questions that will help their clients discover their own answers. You can use the same coach approach. When that inner voice starts talking, ask it some questions that will help you instead of getting in your way. How to do that? Be curious. Let's imagine you are nervous about a presentation you have to give at work in front of the boss and shareholders. Your inner critic starts going wild. "You aren't qualified," it says. "You aren't a very good speaker." So that is the negative stuff.

Now think about that voice being your wise, intuitive, loving voice that wants the best for you. What would it say if you asked for help and support?

Try this, for example: "What can I do to make sure this presentation is a success?" That wise voice will have the answers for you. Perhaps: "Make sure you are prepared" or "Try it out on others before you do it live" or "Get a good night's sleep the night before" or "Get some help with your PowerPoint design" Tap into that intuitive, wise part of your mind and ask for the answers. It knows the answers and knows what to do.

Your internal world – the reality that you encounter within your mind and emotions – is a world that only you can control and create. Your experience is up to you. All of those choices affect your capacity to find your personal overtone.

SECTION FIVE
Overtone Leadership

A re leaders born or made? There is probably no organizational or human development topic more hotly discussed than "What makes a good leader?" My coaching clients are constantly asking me how they can build their leadership capacity and grow their leadership skills. My gut sense is that we have made this discussion of leadership something mystical, and far too complex.

This section pulls apart the myth that leadership is something "out there" and firmly brings the discussion back to "in here." Overtone leadership begins from the inside out.

Leadership is less a set of skills or a role than a way of being. Understanding, believing, and fully stepping into our leadership capacity, begins with the genuine desire to look at self. Leadership begins and ends with each one of us and our individual commitment to understanding our values, vision, motivation, strengths, and blind spots.

If generative leadership is as simple as showing up authentically and acting from that place of congruency, then everyone can be a leader. You don't have to be leading the cavalry down the hill in an attack to be an inspirational and motivational leader. A mother is a leader as she coaxes her reluctant child to let go of her hand on the first day of school. Your neighbor is a leader as she organizes a "raise the rent" party for someone in need. Your friend is a leader when he rallies the community together for a bike ride to raise money for Parkinson's disease research.

"Leadership does not exist in a vacuum. It always operates in context, in relationship. While leaders may lead by virtue of who they are, leaders also create value by virtue of their relationships." [1]
—Kevin Cashman, *Leadership from the Inside Out*

There's a beautiful paradox here. We have to look deeply at the "I" to be an authentic leader. Yet we must connect deeply with the "We" to lead. Are you up for it? Read on.

Chapter 15
BEING THE LEADER

"Leadership is not a job description – it is being… in action."[1]
—Michael Stratford, transformational leadership coach

How do we *be* a leader? In Section Three, we began our overtone journey by establishing a rock-solid foundation: identifying and deeply connecting with our values, guiding principles, and strengths. Aligning these with self, and being willing to commit to a lifelong quest for personal mastery, is the critical starting point.

Developing self-awareness is crucial to a leader's positive development. Self-awareness begins with an honest, deep self-appraisal of values and attitudes, emotional and physical strengths, vulnerabilities, holdbacks, and blind spots. We must suspend self-judgment and be open to new possibilities.

By paying ongoing attention to self, we can increase our capacity and contribute more to the common good. This quest is not a self-focused, narcissistic one – all of our journeying to find our overtone is ultimately for an "other" purpose. Great leaders put that over personal gain or their own agenda. They recognize that there is a greater piece than their own ego. Leaders lead with an understanding of their own and their organization's why.

Your way of being in the world and your commitment to personal mastery is the most pivotal influencer as leader. You must be the change.

"There's nothing more powerful you can do to encourage others in their quest for personal mastery than to be serious in your own quest." [2]
—Peter Senge, *The Fifth Discipline*

Whether you're leading as a CEO, a not-for-profit board member, a choral director, a parent, or a friend, there is nothing more powerfully influential you can do than to practice what you preach. Much as we inspire those around us to express their deepest potential, so must we consciously and consistently attend to the expression of our own potential.

The influence you can impart as a leader from a modeling perspective is profound. "Walking the talk" is a twist on an old phrase that is appropriate here. Besides the obvious positive example of modeling the behavior you want, walking your talk builds trust. I may well have called this entire chapter *Trust* because that is the most important characteristic for a leader to develop with his or her staff or team.

Trust forms the foundational building block of any successful relationship. Trust has to spread throughout an organization – from leader outward, from the front line to senior executives, and from team member to team member. You need to trust the people, the process, and the systems. And yes, you even need to trust yourself. The authenticity with which you approach your work as leader and your consistency of words and actions will build trust. With trust as the foundation for building relationships, you can really begin to move into overtone leadership.

As you can probably sense, all of this overtone work is intimately intertwined. When there is a clear vision aligned with strong values, and a leader who lives those values consistently in word and deed, trust is built on a foundation that ensures resiliency when tough times occur. Resiliency ensures that even with a slight slip, the complete relationship will not be eroded but instead will be merely a brief wobble.

One of the most talked about leadership qualities is charisma. Is charisma something that one is born with, or is one able to cultivate it?

Merriam —Webster defines charisma as:

1: a personal magic of leadership arousing special popular loyalty or enthusiasm

2: a special magnetic charm or appeal

I believe charisma is an energy that exudes from those who acknowledge and live their signature strengths while being confidently aligned with their foundational elements of values and vision. Leaders with charisma share many similar characteristics. They are passionate, positive, generative, and energetic. They value people and can see their greatness. They encourage the best in people and are not limited by comparison or jealousy. They give hope. Although they don't ignore current reality, they are able to see the possibilities and paint the picture of that vision vividly, therefore engaging those around them.

Leaders with charisma are generous in sharing their wisdom and drawing out the best in others. They celebrate those around them and their greatest triumph is a team triumph. Ego is checked at the door. A generative growth mindset would say that charisma is a blend of learnable qualities; we all have the capacity to be charismatic.

We have tossed away the notion of the boss having to be the tough, unmovable person with the answers. Allowing oneself to not know all the answers, or to make mistakes and own them actually creates trust and is part of moving toward personal mastery. Feeling vulnerability, accepting it, and learning from it, opens our leadership capacity.

Overtone leaders approach leadership with a growth mindset, believing that they and their teams have the capacity to develop through learning.

"A good leader inspires people to have confidence in their leader. A great leader inspires people to have confidence in themselves." [3]
—Eleanor Roosevelt

An overtone leader leads with intention. Your intention sets everything in motion. There is no randomness in overtone leadership. Leading with purposeful inspired action will focus and expand your energy, amplify your results, empower you, and increase your resilience. Though you have high intention, you also are not attached to your results. An attachment to results will take you out of the power of the present moment, and an overtone can only exist in the present moment. Lead with high intention and low attachment.

REFLECTION OPPORTUNITY

Best leaders of your life

Think of the best leaders you have had in your life. What qualities did they exude?

Leadership *BEING* Awareness Reflection

Where would you place yourself (with no judgment) on a scale of 1 to 10 in the following areas?

- ☐ Vulnerability – I am willing to emotionally expose myself, be uncertain, be okay with relaxing the "knowing" muscle
- ☐ Intention – I show up with purpose
- ☐ Authenticity – I am real, and aligned with my values
- ☐ Collaborative – I am a team player
- ☐ Communication – I am a proactive communicator and listen deeply
- ☐ Self-awareness – I am willing to look at and explore self
- ☐ Consistency – I am consistent in thought, word, and deed
- ☐ Openness – I am willing to explore new ideas and directions that aren't my own
- ☐ Transparency – I proactively provide information to aid understanding
- ☐ Trust – I trust myself, my colleagues, my board, my shareholders, and my relationships

Add an asterisk beside the area that you feel you might have some growth potential.

Chapter 16
THE ROLE OF A LEADER SIMPLIFIED

"Real leadership is the process of empowering others by abdicating one's power over them. It means to set others free to become all they can be in an atmosphere of innovation and mutual respect." [1]
—Denis Waitley, best-selling author and success coach

The biggest thing a leader can do to be a generative leader and inspire a group to find their overtone is to unwaveringly commit to the exploration of who they *be*. They must commit to their personal mastery journey (Chapter 12), acknowledge their own growing edges with honesty and vulnerability, and courageously and authentically stand in their being.

There has been a big shift and a new understanding about what makes a great leader. The outdated model of an authoritative, command-and-control leader with a top-down hierarchal style is no longer favored. Team members want to be engaged and empowered. They want to feel like their voice matters, and they want autonomy to do their jobs without the leader's interference.

That outdated star leadership model has not only proven to be unsustainable, it also has had repercussions in member disengagement, inefficiencies, low productivity, and high employee turnover. The new desired leadership style is a more collaborative one of servant leadership, where the power is shared and the leader helps the team develop and grow to maximize performance potential. Members of the team have responsibility for their results, feel a connection to the organization's vision and values, participate without fear, trust each other, and are acknowledged for their contributions. Leaders begin by being warm, authentic humans, and inspiring real trust-based connections with the team.

How does this new style of generative leadership connect with the actual role of the leader? The simplicity of this new style makes the leaders I work with gasp excitedly!

The best way for leaders to create an overtone for their team is simply to *allow* their people to be the best they can be. Leaders are there to set the environment and space for success and then step out of the way. They are there to provide a supportive, collaborative, and mentoring presence. They develop the talent and are the guide on the side - not the sage on the stage.

The Role of a Leader Simplified
To create an environment in which the individual talents of the team can flourish and shine to their full potential.

Overtone leadership is all about leaders showing up in their full authentic self and focusing their energies on creating the space for the team to flourish. An overtone leader then nurtures and builds on the strengths of the team while supporting and acknowledging them. By creating and developing the conditions for everyone's talents to flourish and shine to their full potential, leaders have the best chance of creating that extra note – finding the overtone of the organization. By going beyond self and making it about what will help everyone else grow and thrive ... that is being a real leader.

That is Overtone Leadership.

Chapter 17
INTRINSIC INSPIRATION

"You get the best efforts from others not by lighting a fire
beneath them, but by building a fire within them." [1]
—Bob Nelson, best-selling author

The question of how to keep employees or a team motivated has always gotten a lot of attention from leaders. When I think of a leader motivating me, I get a visual of externally imposed action designed to ignite my energy. I think of a sports coach pumping me up from the sidelines, my friends cheering me on at the 7k mark of my first 10k race, or my chorus director boosting our pre-performance enthusiasm. As a leader, external motivation serves a wonderful short-term purpose; however, if we want an approach for long-term sustainable buy-in, we will want to inspire ourselves and our teams from the inside out.

Generative leadership inspires with a connection to the deepest core of who we are. Building on our work in personal mastery, the change begins within. When it comes from that core place and connects with a strong foundation of purpose, values, and vision, it becomes much more than motivating the troops to achieve a goal. It becomes an authentic, aligned, and connected journey into our overtone.

"Carrots and sticks are so last century," said Daniel H. Pink, in his brilliant book, *DRIVE – The Surprising Truth About What Motivates Us.* Pink was referring to the common "carrot and stick" reward-and-punishment motivational technique that most of us grew up with, wherein good behavior is rewarded and poor behavior is punished. Pink refers instead to three essential elements of true motivation (autonomy, mastery, and purpose) that connect to create the most powerful form of motivation – intrinsic motivation – that which comes from within.[2]

Going even further than intrinsic motivation – if one is then *inspired* from within, one will be consistently motivated to achieve.

> *"Motivation is an external, temporary high that pushes you forward. inspiration is a sustainable internal glow which pulls you forward."* [3]
> —Thomas Leonard, founding father of professional coaching

Internal vs. External

As we discussed, external motivation is a good way to get a quick result in the moment. External motivation pushes you to do something.

Think about inviting change instead of imposing it, and watch the shift as your team generates change energy from within. That way, change is not imposed, it is accessed. It can begin with a very subtle language shift. For example, instead of "Ok Team, we need to start thinking outside the parameters of what we have always done," experiment with "Ok Team, I invite you to think outside the parameters of what we have always done. What could that look like?"

When we can build a fire within our constituents, and connect to what is most important to them, it allows them to inspire their own greatness. Remember that your role as leader is to create the atmosphere or conditions for your teams to live into their potential. You aren't there to make it happen. What could connect to the core of who your team is and what they want? Think both personally and as a leader about what will connect with your GPS. Then, do the work to align and instill a connection with that purpose. Move from external motivation to internal inspiration.

Positive vs. Negative

"Fear is a great motivator," my director colleague laughingly tells me. And yes it is, in the short term. Negative motivation and focusing on the costs of not doing something does motivate us to take immediate action. Our brain's emotional center strongly activates our physical response to hightail it out of the forest when we see a bear. Yes, we get out of danger, but we also raise our stress hormone levels and the results aren't pretty. Mental interference is created with fear and there is a shutdown of the learning centers that connect with insight and growth. Even a bit of threat can close down the parts of the brain needed to move ahead. As Daniel Pink said, the punishment-and-reward system is so last century.[4]

> **For a sustainable possibility of working in our overtone,
> we want to shift from negative external motivation
> to positive internal inspiration.**

Obligation vs. Opportunity

Do you usually think of the downside or the cost of not doing something as a way to push you into action? You might ask, "Who cares? If the motivation (negative or otherwise) prompts me into action, doesn't that serve the same purpose and won't that have the same result?"

Well, yes, you may be prompted into action, but much like acting out of fear, you would be acting from a place of scarcity, a limiting attitude, and diminished energy. Your results and your joy factor could be much more positive if you flipped into an opportunity mindset, one of abundance and possibility.

Approach your activities from a place of opportunity vs. obligation with a "What is the opportunity here?" mindset rather than a "What is the cost if I don't do this?" mindset. Examples:

- obligation mindset: "I should go to that networking meeting. If I don't, I might be seen as not being a part of the community."
- opportunity mindset: "If I go to this networking meeting I might meet someone with whom I might want to collaborate."

The weight of obligation is heavy. Feel the burden lift off your shoulders as you step into a situation from a place of curiosity and possibility, instead of one of obligation.

Chapter 18
THERE WILL ALWAYS BE
A *BITSY FAIRHAVEN*

A s a leader, you have dug deep, committed to your journey to personal mastery, set a rock-solid foundation, inspired your teams, and shown up fully and authentically. Everything is in place, your team is empowered, and you are ready. The implementation of the new program that will move you toward achieving your overtone is imminent. Suddenly a voice pipes up and challenges you, a voice of dissent, a non-complier, a complainer, a negative disruptive force. Your confidence, planning, and focus get distracted or derailed. You have just fallen prey to the Pareto Principle, more commonly known as the 80/20 rule.

Vilfredo Pareto, an Italian economist in the 1800s, discovered that 80% of the land in Italy was owned by 20% of the population. Since then, this concept of disproportion has applied to almost every industry and environment. For example, 20% of time expended on something produces 80% of results; 80% of the problems can be attributed to 20% of the causes; 80% of a company's sales come from 20% of its products, and 80% of your phone calls go to 20% of the names on your list, etc.

Although I have taken liberties with adapting this 80/20 principle, and have no empirical studies proving that this principle pertains to human compliance, I propose that with any group or team, especially those of a larger size, there will always be those who just don't get on board with the program. Though a small percentage of the entire group, those people demand a high percentage of energy and cause the majority of the problems. It may not work out to be exactly an 80/20 percentage, but that smaller percentage will demand a disproportionate amount of your attention.

Even if they are not actively resisting, their lack of support or negativity gets in your way as leader. I have named that outlier *Bitsy Fairhaven*. And, my friends, there will *always* be a Bitsy Fairhaven. (Or two or three Bitsys.) Bitsy is the one complaining about the payroll system on her coffee break … Bitsy is the one who doesn't get her report in on time … Bitsy is the one in your chorus who doesn't meet the musical qualification deadlines … Bitsy is the one who sits there with arms crossed, scowling at your project presentation … Bitsy is the persistently negative voice on your staff team … You know the type. I can tell you that I have experienced a Bitsy Fairhaven in every leadership position I have held.

I am amazed time and time again by the profound ways that I and other committed, generative leaders are thrown off our game by one person, or a small percentage of outliers. We spend an inordinate amount of time, energy (and coaching dollars) on ways to get those people on board. An immense amount of mental bandwidth goes toward appealing, cajoling, persuading, strategizing, and basically bending over backward to bring a Bitsy onside.

So What?

We wouldn't even care about Bitsy except that she does interfere with our ability to create an organization overtone. If her effect was neutral, or minimal, we wouldn't care as much – she would simply be an annoyance, a small stone in our shoe. However, Bitsy *does* have an effect on others who encounter her. Perhaps most dramatically, she affects us as leaders. The effect may simply be one of wasted time, diminished focus, or it might be a mental energy-sapper that derails us completely and stays with us for days. As leaders, when we become unaligned and taken out of our zone, we unwittingly affect the other 80% who *are* on board.

We approach our work as leaders by operating from a place of wanting to provide value and do what is best for the team or company. When someone is not onside with that, it generally bothers us and gets in the way. After all, we have the bigger picture in mind with what is best for the group or organization … so why would anyone not get on board?

Guess what? Bitsy doesn't care what you think – Bitsy is focused on Bitsy.

Keep in mind, Bitsy doesn't always have to be a problem. In fact, Bitsy can provide a voice of reality or check to our zealous proposal that can be useful.

However, sometimes it's simply our reaction to Bitsy – and our obsession about having to get Bitsy onside – that hurts us the most.

WHAT TO DO ABOUT BITSY

Option 1 Choose Your Thoughts

> *"Sit back and relax, or sit upright and be uptight. Your choice."*
> —WestJet pilot announcement to passengers onboard
> a plane that was experiencing departure delays

Let's say that you are rolling out a new operational program that will move your organization into achieving your overtone and Bitsy doesn't like it. In fact, she is not shy about expressing her negative opinion. What do you do?

As you begin to get pulled into a Bitsy downward spiral, first ask yourself, "Do I have to bring Bitsy on side? Is having her onside critical to the success of the project? Is Bitsy negatively affecting the rest of the group?"

Then ask yourself, "Am I feeling a need to prove to Bitsy that I am right? Is there a possibility that a converted Bitsy might be the linchpin that moves the group forward?"

These are important questions to ask yourself so that you can then make a choice. As an overtone leader, where do you put your focus? On the outliers? Or those who are on board? Which choice will create less mental interference for you and your team and get you back to your sweet spot? What would have the most generative impact and have the best possibility of moving you forward?

Option 2 Give Bitsy an MRI
(Most Respectful Interpretation)

> *Don't be too quick to attribute questionable motivations to people's actions.*
> *Most of us just don't think far enough ahead to be that devious."* [1]
> —Shaun Belding, Performance Training Consultant

Take a breath and imagine giving Bitsy an MRI. An MRI is a Most Respectful Interpretation.[2] If you give someone the benefit of the doubt and consciously choose an MRI, you open the door to possibility where there wasn't any before. Creating an MRI is a choice, (there's that word again), and by consciously choosing an MRI, you create the possibility of a different outcome.

Let's use the example above. Bitsy is not on board with a new program you are rolling out and doesn't hesitate to voice her opinion.

What MRI could you create? (You do not need to know this is true, it is just a possibility that may be underneath her resistance)

1. Bitsy is scared that the new program will mean more work for her.

2. Bitsy is worried that the new program will cause the organization to lose so much money that other programs she runs will be cut.

3. Bitsy has some serious personal challenges right now that are clouding her perspective.

Imagine that any of those MRIs are true. How does holding the space for those as possibilities for Bitsy shift your outlook?

Option 3 Use Your Overtone Foundation as Support

Use your rock solid foundation as a platform upon which to have a discussion with Bitsy. If your organizational values and cultural practices are clear, you can talk to Bitsy about her actions or point of view from that place, instead of a personal "You don't agree with me" place. If the company value is say, *teamwork*, one could begin the discussion from that place of orientation.

A group I coached had a Bitsy who was overheard loudly saying negative things about the leader to others in a public space. Bitsy was upset at what she perceived as a personal slight caused by a decision the leader had made and was vocalizing her displeasure to anyone who would listen. Having a conversation with Bitsy that centered on the group's stated values of *loyalty* and *respect* offered a non-judgmental perspective. Using the group's values as a framework helped both parties have a constructive and open discussion leading to better understanding.

REFLECTION OPPORTUNITY

When you get thrown off as leader by a Bitsy ask yourself...

1. If Bitsy doesn't comply, what would the outcome be?
2. Is Bitsy affecting others on the team, or solely me?
3. Is Bitsy standing in the way of results? Progress? Productivity?
4. What is the reason I am so affected by Bitsy?
5. What is an MRI I could give Bitsy?
6. How is Bitsy affecting my Overtone Leadership?
7. What will help me keep my focus on the other 80%?
8. Who can support me in keeping on track?

SECTION SIX
Overtones for Organizations

We have examined what you can do as an individual and as a leader to create the foundation and conditions most conducive to creating the Overtone Effect.

When is the best time to start the work to discover your organization overtone? The answer is: Right here, right now. "Aw, but we should have thought about this before and started this years ago," you might say. I recommend you stop the "should-ing." It is not generative! You can begin this overtone process at any time if you are willing and committed and open to change.

How then does one create a generative mindset and will in an entire organization? The process is essentially the same as finding your personal overtone. You have been given a lot of tools already in this book to work from an individual level to discover your values and guiding principles, and it is important to understand how those align with those held by your organization or team.

Glossing over any of the foundational steps, or omitting the all-important full involvement of every person, will negate the possibility of your organization finding its overtone.

Bear in mind, this takes time. It takes will and a commitment from the very top for it to be truly successful. It takes energy and openness to change. The process takes patience and it is not a set-and-forget process. It will flex, grow, and shift, and you must be open to adapting and revisiting it over time.

As you read this section, although I use the word 'organization', you can insert the words 'team', 'company', 'chorus', or 'quartet' anywhere along the way, as the principles apply to all groups.

Chapter 19
THE SOUND OF YOUR ORGANIZATION

"Music is the wine which inspires one to new generative processes." [1]
—Ludwig van Beethoven

E very organization has a unique "sound." It is a collection of its attitudes, experiences, history, beliefs, and values, all of which guide programs, processes, and decisions.

The parts making up your sound are your differentiators and can cause you to soar and stand out boldly. Identifying your signature differentiators and stepping fully into them can move you further toward your organization overtone – that sweet spot of flow where the results transcend the work. Chances are if you're not in tune with your organization's sound, it's working against you.

The first step to finding your organization overtone is to identify who you are, what you are, and where you are. How do you operate? What is important to you? What are the things that make your organization unique or different? Do this research with the learning lens of a scientist, using curiosity and suspending judgment as you gather the data with full member input.

The work to find the sound of your organization is similar to that of the work you did to find and align your individual overtone. Adopt a generative approach, mindset and language, and begin the work by building, revisiting, or revitalizing your overtone foundation. Define your values and strengths. You will need full openness and awareness to be able to achieve your organization overtone. The individuals and the collective voices need to be heard, aligned, and balanced to create an organization overtone.

As you do this work, be sure your leader/CEO brings high-quality personal attention to this process. This is an intentional process, done with purpose and passion, connection and openness (See Section Five). All voices must be heard. Working together in perfect harmony is what creates the possibility for an overtone.

Organizations are ever changing, and to remain resilient, the foundation and the core of who they are must be clear and strong. When you shift too far away from the center (by design, or accident, or simply inattention), you run into trouble.

Lions Gate Chorus experienced unexpected success in the International a cappella Chorus Competition in 2007, jumping from a twelfth place ranking to third place bronze medalists. We rode that energy into the next International competition and placed second with a silver medal, also winning the Most Entertaining Chorus award. In the subsequent two International competitions we stayed in the Top Five, but oddly, the experiences were not filled with the same freedom and joy; instead they felt like a more arduous process of striving to win. It started to become clear that we had drifted too far from our organizational center – the core of who we really were. We had inadvertently started trying to be who we thought we needed to be to win the gold medal.

That realization kick-started leadership discussions and a commitment to extensive work in defining who we are and who we want to be as we continue our journey in the pressure-filled high levels of competition. We began this intense exploration with the data collected in a survey that had an astounding 96% participation rate from our membership. The survey asked provocative in-depth questions to help us dig deep into who we were and what we wanted.

The revitalization process hasn't always been comfortable – but we have persisted. Rediscovering our unique organizational sound has helped focus operations and programs based on alignment with our core values. We are embracing and celebrating who we really are and leveraging and building from our strengths.

Do the deep-dive work to discover and define who you are, what you stand for, and what makes you unique – your difference-makers. Then, align your members and programs with that core sound to keep you in your organizational sweet spot and help set up the possibilities for finding your overtone.

Chapter 20
CULTURE BY DESIGN

There is a lot of talk these days about creating "culture shift" in organizations. The culture of an organization is a combination of the attitudes, experiences and values that guide the behavior of the members. It really means who we are, and how we do everything.

Organizations often have a culture by happenstance rather than a culture by design. Without intentionally creating the foundation and supports for the culture they want, what happens haphazardly becomes the norm.

By contrast, the generative approach would have you intentionally create and design the culture that fits with your foundational bricks (See Section Three). Having a common guiding purpose, a clear and communicated vision, and clarity about shared values throughout the entire organization, will increase buy-in, engagement, trust, and respect. It will also promote the alignment needed for your overtone to exist.

When we look at our organizations through a lens of determining what it is we want to create, without limitation, (See the *Thinking Outside the Dot* exercise in Chapter 9) we begin to sense where the energy, the sound, and the driving pulse of our organization lies. Intentionally linking that vision with values and purpose will create a solid base for culture shift or revitalization.

Healthy generative cultures that intentionally connect the values and purpose of the organization with those of the individual create meaning and a sense of purpose. They pave the way for individuals to connect to something bigger than self, and that fosters an atmosphere where an overtone can flourish. That alignment will have a positive impact and result in deeper member engagement, commitment, better morale, efficiency, and results.

In Chapter 4 we learned to adopt a growth mindset[1] in order to find our overtone. A growth mindset will help us tap into, capitalize on, and maximize the talents of our members to create a more positive and engaged organization. A culture supporting a fixed mindset focuses solely on demonstrating skills and being good at all times. A growth mindset has a consistent focus on developing the skills to make things better.

A growth mindset benefits:
- Creativity and innovation
- Resilience
- Persistence
- Superior performance
- Well-being

There are several ways to foster a growth mindset in an organization. Some of them include:
- Encouraging experimentation
- Focusing on progress over time vs. a finite moment
- Putting markers in place to measure improvement
- Celebrating growth and each signpost on the journey
- Giving opportunities to improve and offering support for those opportunities at every level of the organization
- Senior leaders modeling their commitment to ongoing learning

Challenge yourself and your leadership team – what mindset do you believe is true and most important?

The Song of Atlanta Show Chorus[2] (SOA) is an accomplished 100-person chorus, which had easily and consistently won their Regional a cappella chorus competition for almost thirty years. They had further success by advancing to become the fourth place medalists in the prestigious International competition. They were excited to be on the rise to the top.

Then, in 2013, the chorus experienced a crisis when they unexpectedly came in second place in their regional competition for the first time ever. A lot of intense soul-searching went on as they reeled in the aftermath. Fingers were pointed, and blame was levied. At the end of the day, SOA's charismatic director, Becki Hine, along with her strong and stable musical leadership team, took responsibility, reached out for coaching support, and started to rebuild the new SOA.

Starting with a pulse-check exercise done with sticky notes, Becki allowed space for each member to share what they were feeling, with the safety of anonymity. She then took the members back to a time when they were successful and asked what was happening then.

Not only did they find out where they were starting from – they also found out where they wanted to move to, and what they were willing to do to get there. Becki continued with a values exercise that was a huge confidence and unity builder. It was then that the chorus discovered the incredible alignment they had with the core of who they were and what was important to them.

The mood and culture started to shift quickly, and is still shifting. As Becki reflected, "It's a scary thing to realize you can't make the shift by yourself … You can take steps to encourage it but you can't change it by yourself." As we touched on earlier with our Dalai Lama story, change has to happen from within. Becki is a courageous leader and was willing and committed to making changes to how she showed up, yet Becki alone was unable to make the shift for her chorus. The will had to be there for each member to begin making the required shifts. Her leadership modeling was a generative opener for others to step up and start taking some of the responsibility from this "star leader" and own it for themselves. The chorus is now happy, healthy and actively moving forward to live into their organization's overtone.

"Unless leaders choose to shift, the collective purpose is not fulfilled." [3]
—Janet Harvey, Master Certified Coach

Where There's Will...

Carollyne Conlinn[4] is one of the founding partners of Essential Impact Coaching Inc., which has created coaching cultures in organizations worldwide and has been lauded for its seminal culture shift work. Since the International Coach Federation created the Global Prism Awards ten years ago, Essential Impact has received the revered top honor twice.

Carollyne stresses there must be a baseline willingness for any organization to make a shift. There has to be a compelling vision and a desire to make change. Perhaps you may not want or need a complete culture shift, maybe you are simply looking for revitalization. Perhaps you are revisiting your core foundation and getting more intentional about work you completed years earlier. Whatever your desired result, you must start with a vision for that change.

Carollyne says the process is different for each organization and one must apply real attention to detail in the change process. Shifting organizational culture is a fluid, ever-changing, and organic process. As conditions change, one must be flexible and adaptive to improve on the plan while keeping true to the original vision. To create a new overtone for an organization undergoing a culture shift, the foundational elements must be in place and there must be alignment of the operating systems with the human processes.

The culture shift process is holistic, and Carollyne says that working through the entire process can take three to five years. Though it is not an overnight process, and involves a considerable investment of time and energy, the sustainable benefits of undertaking this pivotal work can be astounding, and can have far-reaching and measurable results.

Chapter 21
OVERTONE TOOLS: CREATING AN
ACKNOWLEDGMENT-RICH CULTURE

G iving deep acknowledgment is one of the most powerful tools you and your team have for setting an environment conducive to creating an overtone. The benefits of consistent, authentic appreciation go much further than giving a nice warm fuzzy feeling. An acknowledgment-rich culture results in greater happiness, growth, employee retention, and satisfaction.

Studies done at the corporate level hold that being appreciated is more important to employees than salary and working conditions.[1]

- 87% of job seekers report the Number One characteristic they desire in a workplace is to feel valued.
- 79% of the employees who quit their job cited lack of appreciation as a key reason for their leaving.

People quite simply respond to authentic acknowledgment. If you and your team incorporate deep acknowledgment into your day-to-day business strategy, you will almost instantly create a generative culture that will move you closer to achieving your overtone.

Rob recently retired after thirty-four years of service in a senior management position at a large corporation. There were a series of parties held in his honor, and in a subsequent coaching session, Rob couldn't stop talking about the amazing things his bosses and colleagues had said to him both privately and publicly. Sure, they mentioned his stellar work performance, but more importantly, they talked about his character, his personality, his strengths, and his commitment. In short, they gave him deep acknowledgment for the person he was, not just what he had done. That acknowledgment was far more valuable and impactful to Rob than the receipt of that very nice gold watch.

Generally we only get this kind of deep acknowledgment at some big life event such as a retirement, and sadly, we don't hear the words often enough during our lifetime. The one time we *can* count on people waxing poetic about who we are is when they deliver our eulogy. (It's too bad we aren't around to hear it!)

Imagine the importance of deep acknowledgment in a member-driven organization where salaries or other tangible benefits are not considerations to continuing membership.

This is a challenge in any kind of culture with exacting standards of excellence, where nothing is ever fully realized. It has been a constant concern of the high-achieving musical directors I coach that if they acknowledge people for *x* when they didn't do *y* or *z*, those people will get complacent and think that's good enough. Others subscribe to old school ways of thinking with beliefs like "They know they are good, I don't have to acknowledge them" or "Too much praise waters down all acknowledgment. It will be more meaningful if I don't show my appreciation too often." Do any of those statements sound familiar?

I guarantee that if you have created your overtone foundation, if you have a clear vision with aligned values, and if your people know, believe, and subscribe to the organization's GPS, the acknowledgment of one step on the way will not stop them in their tracks. Instead, it will inspire them to keep going. They will understand that acknowledgment of one signpost on the road does not mean that the journey has ended.

Baseline Ingredients: Recognize and Appreciate Regularly

"Don't forget, a person's greatest emotional need is to feel appreciated." [2]
—H. Jackson Brown Jr., author

Let's start first with recognition or appreciating people for a job well done. Most of us have become comfortable with giving recognition and remembering to say thank you. Yay us!

Generally the quick rah-rah type of recognition such as, "Great work on the Hardy case, Laura" or "Nice job on the flyer layout, Sam" is unmemorable, easily forgotten, and doesn't last long. Still, any kind of recognition is a good thing, so be sure to continue the bonuses, high fives, and employee-of-the-month recognitions. We must continue to celebrate and recognize people for the work they do. A paycheck is never enough.

And certainly in both volunteer-based organizations and corporations, we have to treat the people doing the jobs with gratitude and thanks. Each of us wants to know our contribution is appreciated and makes a difference.

How to Make Recognition More Powerful

Be Specific

To make recognition more powerful, be as specific as you can. A blanket "Way to go, Marketing Team" is less effective than "Way to go Marketing Team – your social media strategies were innovative and really captured the public's interest."

Or, to use the previous examples above, consider: "Great work on the Hardy case, Laura. That was a tough one and you were so well prepared the defense couldn't possibly counter" or "Nice job on the flyer layout, Sam. It really makes our marketing message pop."

Detail the pieces that gave the work value and prompted the recognition.

Be Consistent and Recognize Frequently

Appreciate and recognize your staff or members consistently, and communicate regularly. Deliver the appreciation personally. It goes without saying that a few customized words from the boss delivered to you alone will land deeper than a blanket email sent to several people. And no, hitting the Facebook "Like" button is never enough. At best, that's merely a "push pin acknowledgment" – a quick pin-point hit. Make it personal.

Be Authentic

Most of all, the recognition must be authentic. As a leader, if that feels uncomfortable and is a growing edge for you, then get some coaching to help you work on it.

Recognition and Appreciation are not Enough – Add the Secret Sauce of Deep Acknowledgment

Frequent and specific recognition and appreciation is not enough. For an even greater positive impact and a profound route to creating an overtone, learn and practice how to give deep acknowledgment.

Acknowledgement goes beyond what a person did, and notices what it is about the person that allowed them to do what they did. When we deeply acknowledge, we see the person...not just the action. It is a deep desire of everyone to be seen, heard and understood, and since acknowledgment goes much deeper, it has a more powerful impact on the person receiving it.

> *"Remind people who they are*
> *instead of just complimenting*
> *them on what they've done."* [3]
> —Thomas Leonard

Practicing deep acknowledgment on a daily basis has dramatic benefits in both professional and personal settings. Acknowledgment can inspire, deepen connections, increase performance, open possibilities, and bring joy. Heck, receiving deep acknowledgment just plain feels good!

Although at first it might feel awkward to give deep acknowledgment, keep at it. You will find that giving that kind of deep acknowledgment fills you with more positive emotions and feeds on itself. It is a rewarding feeling to see the impact you can bring. Experiment with your work colleagues, with your staff, with your partner, your friends, and your family. Why wait for the eulogy? Use the steps below to experience how the power of deep acknowledgment can transform people while they are still alive.

Five Steps to Giving Deep Acknowledgment

1. Set the stage

Feeling at ease with giving deep acknowledgment is a skill to be nurtured. Many of us also need to learn how to comfortably *receive* deep acknowledgment. Public acknowledgment can be overwhelming. Be sensitive to the recipient, the timing, and the environment in which you give acknowledgment.

2. Acknowledge the person for who they are

Go beyond their performance and highlight specific qualities in the person that showed up in what they did: commitment, caring, thoughtfulness, creativity, initiative, enthusiasm, etc.

3. Make it short and sweet

Keep your acknowledgment simple and to the point. A shorter statement can often be easier to receive, and therefore has greater impact.

4. Be real

Speak honestly from the heart no matter how uncomfortable you may feel. The authenticity will deepen the impact. Not feeling it? Then don't say it. Deep acknowledgment must be sincere.

5. Give it freely and let it land

Give acknowledgment freely, without expectation of a response. Be prepared for the person receiving the acknowledgment to deflect your comments. "Oh it was nothing – really it was a team triumph." A diffident teenager may even leave the room!

If your acknowledgment does get brushed off, you might add another layer to your deep acknowledgment. In the example above you could add: "Yes, I agree – the entire team was brilliant and pulled together beautifully. I really want to acknowledge your role and the calm, organized and inspirational way you kept the team together. Thank you."

Adding a natural end to the conversation like 'thank you' can allow the person receiving to more easily accept the acknowledgment. It can also signal an end to the conversation and allow an easy exit for someone who may be feeling uncomfortable. As I said earlier, be sensitive to the comfort level of the person you are acknowledging so that the acknowledgment lands for them.

Chapter 22
OVERTONE TOOLS: GENERATIVE GROWTH THROUGH FEED FORWARD

Joe took his colleague Sue to lunch to give her some feedback about a recent event she had coordinated. He wanted to talk about where she had messed up and how to improve, but knowing he had to say some good things, he led with some positive comments. He then waited until dessert before he began relaying his criticism. Sue smelled a rat and got defensive and shut down. Joe's potentially valuable input was lost.

I put a lot of attention in my first book, *Harmony from the Inside Out*, on how to make the giving of feedback a positive and generative process instead of a thinly-veiled way of delivering negative criticism. Even when we're coming from an intentional place of wanting the best for the person to whom we're giving feedback, and even if we're using a "feedback sandwich" (with a balance of the positive and critical), my readers called "Foul!" They were convinced that the person giving them feedback was mostly interested in telling them what they did wrong. Even the words "I would like to give you some feedback" was enough threat to shut them down. They viewed balanced feedback with suspicion, and critical feedback with defensiveness.

As staff or team members, however, we do need to know if we are performing up to expected levels. My high-achieving clients *want* to know how they are doing so that they can improve. As leaders we are committed to helping our employees learn and improve their performance.

How best then to have the discussions around those areas of potential improvement – the growing edges?

The very nature of the word feed*back* indicates the giving of an opinion or assessment of something that has already happened. Because feedback occurs after something took place, it is only of use in helping us make changes in the future. Feedback cannot change something that has already happened.

Think about the purpose of giving feedback. I would hope that anyone reading this would be giving feedback with the intention of wanting the person to perform differently/improve in the future, rather than making them feel bad about the deficiencies of their work. There is no currency in telling someone what they did wrong or focusing on the past unless it clearly helps to identify what you want them to shift.

In a generative culture, with a growth mindset, we approach what we do with a desire to improve, to grow, to excel. We focus on moving forward, improving, and growing into our future possibilities rather than staying stuck on our flawed performance in the past.

I say that not as a way to ignore the past, or the things that didn't work, only to point out that focusing on what you did in the past can't change it. By identifying and acknowledging what you want to change, you can create your future.

Feed forward is a concept coined by world-renowned business thinker Marshall Goldsmith.[1] He takes the concept of feedback, and with a slight language shift moves it from a remedial "fixing" of what has already happened into a forward look at the possibilities of what could happen in the future. With the lens of feed forward, the mind expands and creative thought and energy come into motion. Very much aligned with the generative focus outlined in Chapter 3, placement of focus toward what we want in the future instead of what we don't want in the past can liberate opportunity and potential. Feed forward is done with a learner, not a judger mindset.

I once worked in senior management in a large cultural institution where feedback consisted of an annual performance review with a ratings grid. The CEO had given no ongoing feedback on my performance throughout the year and only grudgingly held this annual compulsory performance review session with me. He rated me 3 or 4 out of 5 on all sections of the review with no explanation. When I asked what would make my work a five, he responded that no one gets a five and that if he gave me one I might think I didn't need to work as hard.

How different that annual performance review would have been using a feed forward process. If both people were at the table with a true desire to grow and learn, what kind of conversation might have unfolded?

That story highlights two important points:

1. It is a myth that acknowledging excellent work will cause complacency. Instead, as we saw in our chapter on acknowledgment, praise is a motivational tool. There is no evidence to support the idea that if someone knows they are working at a high level that they will slack off.

2. Feed forward must be an ongoing and important part of working together. The mutuality of the desire to get better, to grow, and to learn together is part of a healthy and generative overtone environment. A once-a-year performance review is never adequate.

How to Give Feed Forward

Pre-work:

- First of all be sure you have fostered a generative culture that holds trust at the core of its foundation.
- Be sure to establish an environment of communication based on consistent and ongoing dialogue to help set the stage for conversation.

Make it a two-way conversation:

Enroll your employee in the mutuality of the exchange.

"People want two-way conversations that pull out their ideas and open their eyes to greater possibilities, not one-way directives focused on what they did wrong." [2]
—Marcia Reynolds, Master Certified
Coach and best-selling author

Feed Forward Conversation Tips:

- Identify where you are now. For example, "That was quite the event. How did that go for you? How are you feeling about it now that it's over?" Or, "Let's talk about the report you handed in, the new marketing plan, the change in your job duties – how do you feel about it?"
- Ask them what they did/are doing well.
- Acknowledge what they did/do well.
- What would they like to improve in the future?
- Let them know what you would like to see in the future.
- Mutually identify areas where the person in front of you could grow to get to that desired future state.
- What do they need to support them moving forward?
- How, as a leader, could you provide support?

Oh, and of course, use your deep acknowledgment skills wherever possible!

SECTION SEVEN
Sustaining Your Overtone

As we have read throughout this book, the Overtone Effect is created by a delicate combination of synchronistic energies coming together in perfect harmony at an exact moment. Sustaining an overtone can be tricky. A host of external or internal factors can cause even a slight non-misalignment that will throw our systems out of balance. Though challenging to sustain, we can, with the system developed in this book, make it easier to find our overtone, live in it more often, and feel the Overtone Effect for longer periods of time.

Challenges and changes are part of our journey to mastery and can be either debilitating blocks or exciting opportunities. In this section we will identify some of the most common challenges to sustaining our overtone, and by using a generative mindset and approach we will examine how to turn these weaknesses or challenges into opportunities for growth. Once we notice the undesired state, we can flip our focus to where we want to move to make change.

Through my coaching of leaders in all industries – from the C-Suite to entrepreneurs, from non-profit leaders to musical directors – I have discovered some common growing edges.

Each of these growth areas deserves a book of their own. Nevertheless, each chapter of this section offer my pithiest talking points for possible generative movement should this be *your* growing edge. This section is also appropriate to groups because each individual can affect the group's ability to find its overtone. Building resiliency capacity, creating balance, establishing boundaries, and caring (without carrying) will help create the space for your overtone to flourish. Addressing these common challenge areas – whichever resonate with you – will help open the pathway for you to find and sustain your overtone.

Chapter 23
BUILDING RESILIENCY

"I've missed more than nine thousand shots in my career. I've lost almost three hundred games. Twenty-six times, I've been trusted to take the game winning shot and missed. I've failed over and over and over again in my life. And that is why I succeed." [1]
—Michael Jordan

Like basketball legend Michael Jordan's description of his career, which wasn't all superstar moments, we all experience challenges or what we might even label as failures in our lives and businesses. Sometimes the mess-ups or disasters come one at a time; sometimes they all seem to land at once. Sometimes there's no one dramatic disaster, it's just a long period of nothing quite working out. We all face challenges; this is reality – it is not a question of *if*, it is only a question of *when*. The very magical essence of our lives includes the full range of experiences – the good, the bad, the ugly, and the beautiful. What is most important is how quickly and fully we can get back on track when beset by challenges.

Building the critical skill of resiliency (how we recover from the setbacks and knockdowns) will positively affect our well-being and success. Resiliency will help us to move more easily through our life challenges and thrive in our overtone state again.

Nancy had worked night and day, and sunk her life savings into her business dream of creating a French-inspired day spa in the heart of Vancouver. After adding the last accent of lavender paint to the walls, she held a 'soft' opening day with friends. The practice workday was filled with people who made appointments and came in for different kinds of treatments so that Nancy could tweak all parts of the operation. She went home excited, fully prepared for next day's Grand Opening event. The phone rang early the next morning. It was her spa manager calling to tell her they had been robbed in the night. Among other equipment and inventory, the brain of the operation, the main computer, was gone.

The initial shock was huge, but Nancy was passionate about her dream. She delayed opening by a day, and operated for a few weeks without the computer until the insurance claim went through. The first year was a nail-biter, and Nancy even had to sell her condo to pay for overhead. It took three years before the spa was profitable.

I surmised it was Nancy's core strengths of tenacity and creativity that kept her thinking of solutions throughout the adversity and challenges of those first years of running her business, but I wondered what else kept her going. In conversation, she told me that she had remained certain and passionate about her dream. People had believed and invested in her and she could not let them down. Her value of personal integrity and unshakeable confidence in her vision would not let her fail. They reminded her that she was successful and current setbacks neither defined her, nor would they destroy her. Her vision remained intact, and that perspective gave her the strength and power to continue. Nancy built the business into a very successful multi-award winning independent day-spa respite in the middle of the city.

FIVE STEPS TO BUILDING RESILIENCY CAPACITY

Step One – Maintain and Grow your Resiliency Bank Account

Think of your Resiliency Capacity as a bank account – your RBA. What is your bank balance? Is it depleted? Overdrawn? In a proactive way you must make a conscious effort to deposit in, restore, and replenish your RBA on an ongoing basis so it is full when you need to make a withdrawal.

How to Fill your Resiliency Bank Account (RBA):

1. Build a Strong Foundation
When you have built a strong foundation for self and team (Section Three), you will automatically be more resilient. Being able to trust and hold on to core values, guiding principles, and vision will help provide solid comfort to inspire the bounce-back capacity you need. Your unique strengths add wealth to keep in your RBA and draw on whenever you feel the need. Once you build that strong foundation you will always have it. Even if the walls tumble down around you, you will still be standing on solid ground and can rebuild.

2. Put Your Own Oxygen Mask on First
Remember that concept from Chapter 13? Make self-value an integral and non-negotiable part of your life. Positive thoughts, sleep, exercise, and nutrition – you know the drill. You have much more capacity to rebound when you make a practice of consciously and consistently valuing your physical, mental, and emotional needs.

3. Create Supports
Who in your life strengthens you? Who gives you the kind of support you want? How can you reach out to them? Learn to accept that although everyone cannot give you everything, different people can each support and contribute to your needs in their unique way. Celebrate those people. In your business, what back-up plans do you have? What supports do you offer your team?

145

4. Find Daily Small Comforts

Identify the little things that might make the most difference for you during challenging periods. They will give you the energy and resiliency to look forward again. Give yourself some daily consistency that is immovable. Having these small comforts gives you a sense of structure and control, and adds to your RBA.

> When Ron was struggling with considerable stress over finding cash to keep his new venture afloat, he gained strength by his morning ritual of sitting down with a heaping bowl of cornflakes soaked in cold milk. That 15-minute cereal routine gave him a solid start of normalcy and calm to begin each day of business pressures.

5. Up your Positivity Ratio

Appreciate and acknowledge yourself and your team. All of this praise and recognition goes into the bank that you and your team can draw upon when there is stress or difficulty.

6. Develop a Gratitude Attitude

Beef up your resiliency bank account daily by adopting a Gratitude Attitude for everything in your life. If you have lost a loved one, remember their life and the good times you shared; celebrate rather than shoving the memories away. If you have had a business setback, remember and celebrate your past successes and acknowledge with gratitude the elements that contributed to those successes. Notice the small things and bless them daily.

7. Create Daily Magic Moments

Once per day *consciously* do something that feeds you.

8. Give yourself a PEP talk

Create a **P**ersonal **E**mpowerment **P**hrase **(PEP)** to recite when you are experiencing a tough time. "I am confident, qualified, and I've got this!" for example. As a reminder, wear a resiliency band (a simple elastic band put around your wrist). Whenever you feel yourself off course, snap your band as a reminder to give yourself a PEP talk.

Step Two – Fully Acknowledge

A friend said something very wise to me after I apologized to her for still being upset a few months after my mom's passing. She said, "Hey, however long you want to talk about your mom and have it be all about you is perfectly fine." She gave me permission and space to grieve.

When you get hit with a crisis, disaster, or setback, it is important to give yourself the space to openly acknowledge and allow full expression of the feelings you are experiencing.

- Actively build some quiet moments into your schedule to give yourself the space you need to feel and process your changing emotions. These blocks of time may arise at different times of the day or week.
- Journal about your feelings.
- Share your feelings with a trusted friend, colleague, or family member.
- Allow yourself full expression of whatever emotions you feel.

When one gets knocked down there is an initial reaction to search for a reason. That may result in blaming something or someone other than ourselves. This is part of the grieving process and precedes the stage in which we accept personal responsibility for our feelings and can begin to move forward.

Whatever the reasons for your knockdown – big or small – if you attempt to avoid your feelings they become amplified and can accelerate a downward spiral that will further hamper your resiliency. Deal with your challenges however you need to. Remember: there is a difference between denial and transcendence.

A group disappointment needs to be addressed in the same fashion as a personal one. Bear in mind that everyone in the group will recover and bounce back at different rates. Give the space and support for everyone to proceed at their own pace in managing the emotional fallout surrounding setbacks or changes.

Step Three – Regain Perspective

All of us get knocked down to varying degrees at different points in our lives. As the drama swirls around you it is easy to lose perspective. Is *everything* messed up? Or, when you take a breath, step back, and really look at your life, is it mostly okay? What do you know to be true that you can hang on to?

Classic illustrations of resiliency (or lack of it) happen frequently in the very public world of professional sports. In golf, where the mental game is of paramount importance, how you recover from a bad shot can be the deciding factor in a tour win accompanied by hundreds of thousands of dollars. Interestingly, there has been a pattern of golfers having superior resilience in tournaments that occur right after they have become fathers. The life-changing experience of having a newborn puts the bad shots into perspective – and that may result in a more consistent emotional level of play.

Perdita Felicien was a Canadian world-champion hurdler, heavily favored to win the gold medal in the 100-meter hurdles at the 2004 Summer Olympics in Athens. The hopes of a nation were on her, expectations were high, and the pressure on her was surely incredible. In the final race, she dramatically hit the first hurdle and fell hard, taking herself out of the race and shattering her Olympic gold medal dreams. She was devastated. She had trained hard for that moment every day for years, and in a heartbeat, the moment was gone.

After reflection, she talked to reporters. "I have learned not to define myself by one event, no matter how big," she said. "My self-worth is not dependent on an event that lasts less than 13 seconds. Hurdling is what I do; it is not what defines me. That is why I know, in this challenging time, I will emerge better (for having struggled) and thrive once again." [2]

Perdita drew on her Resiliency Bank Account to reconnect with her greater purpose to give her the perspective she needed to continue.

Step Four – Hold to Purpose and Look Ahead

When you are ready, revisit your vision, your "Big Picture," your purpose in life – and know that although the circumstances for your knockdown might feel out of your control, making the choice to build on that experience to move forward in a new way is in your control. What future state (emotional, mental, spiritual, or physical) do you want to create? Build on your past successes to create your new vision of what you want to be, do or have. Turn your focus to where you want to go. If you keep your focus on everything you have lost and look for someone to blame, you will remain stuck or enter a downward spiral. Allow that sense of forgiveness to extend to yourself.

"Forgiveness does not change the past, but it does enlarge the future." [3]
—Paul Boese, businessman

Part of resilience is resourcefulness, and if you are open to stepping into an expanded identity and creating a different plan, you can use the energy of the knockdown to spring you upward with the possibility of going even farther and higher than you went before.

Step Five – Make the Choice

You have the power to create your life in the way you want, and in the timeframe you want. Before you get caught up in specific goals and action planning, reignite your passion by dreaming of future possibilities without limits. Then the choice is yours.

"I got half-a-dozen paintings from that shattered plate." [4]
—Georgia O'Keeffe

REFLECTION OPPORTUNITY

Checklist: How to Fill your Resiliency Bank Account

- ☐ I put my own oxygen mask on first.
- ☐ I am getting enough sleep.
- ☐ I am getting fresh air daily.
- ☐ I am physically active daily.
- ☐ I am eating nutritious foods.
- ☐ I am building some quiet reflection time into each day.
- ☐ I know my strengths and positive qualities and remind myself of them daily.
- ☐ I have defined my values and hold to them.
- ☐ I have set up my supports – physical, mental, emotional, and spiritual.
- ☐ I ask for support regularly and accept support easily.
- ☐ I respect and value my needs.
- ☐ I have a daily small comfort that always gives me a sense of normalcy.
- ☐ I have someone with whom to share my feelings.
- ☐ I have developed a gratitude attitude and count my blessings daily.
- ☐ I laugh.
- ☐ I sing.
- ☐ I laugh some more.
- ☐ I celebrate my successes.
- ☐ I have developed my big picture vision and know my "Why".
- ☐ I have a GPS that drives me.
- ☐ I accept help when it is offered.
- ☐ I ask for help when I need it.

Chapter 24
CREATING BALANCE

For more than a decade, Vancouver artist Kent Avery[1] has kept weekend walkers on Vancouver's gorgeous Stanley Park Seawall fascinated with his balancing rock sculptures on the shoreline. Avery deftly balances rocks of radically different sizes and shapes atop one another to create amazing sculptural masterpieces. It seems improbable that such impossibly shaped rocks can balance on each other.

The pieces of our lives are like Avery's rocks. The way they fit together is different for each of us and can be quite miraculous. It is up to each of us to decide on the configuration that is right for us and for our lives.

An overtone is impossible to achieve without balance and alignment. When we think of a visual to represent balance, the image of a scale with two weights comes to mind.

The common phrase "work-life balance" suggests that one side of the scale is work and one side is life. Most often, the weight is imbalanced with the work side tipping the scale with its heavier load. When did we adopt the concept that there is *work* and then there is *life*? I would like to suggest a reframe to this outdated mode of thinking.

The balance we are looking for is a balance within all parts of our life scale. Our work is but one part of our life. Let's move to the concept of there being only one name on the weight, and it's called *Life*. Instead of balance being a measure of work/life, it really means getting clear about what matters to you and then making the conscious choice to align your actions and activities with those priorities. Imbalance happens when you are not aligned.

> *"Balance is not a matter of managing your time or giving equal effort to two opposing sides; it is about aligning your behavior with what you believe is really important to you. When our lives don't reflect our values, we feel that inconsistency as a measure of imbalance."* [2]
> —Joan Gurvis, co-author *Finding your Balance*

Over-focusing in one area of your life is not an issue if it is aligned with your values and what you want for your life. The stress, incongruence, and unhappiness come if imbalance tilts you into a place that is not connected to your core essence. For example, my priority for the past several years has been getting my new coaching business to flourish. Yes, I have been working toward this goal seven days a week, several hours per day. An outsider might look at this with our old scale paradigm and say I am out of balance. However, since I am absolutely doing what I believe is most important to me right now, I do not in any way have the disquieting feeling that comes from being out of balance.

Achieving Balance

Achieving the balance needed to find and live your overtone is a three-part process that involves:

1. Determining what balance you really want in your life.

2. Becoming acutely aware of where you are currently putting your energy and time.

3. Aligning your actions to support your desired overtone balance.

Finding your perfect rock-balancing place will be an ever-changing journey that you will reevaluate constantly and adjust accordingly. Like the rock sculptures, each piece of your life is built on and connected to each other. At the core, there needs to be a solid foundation of your values and life purpose. To keep those rocks standing, you must keep changing and revising, as well as adding some and taking some away. And, you must do all of this while maintaining that strong foundation.

REFLECTION OPPORTUNITY

1. Ask: The first key question to opening up your magical overtone balance is to ask yourself what balance you really want. Thinking with your heart, ask yourself what is really important for your life. Consider categories such as work, social, spiritual, physical, etc.

2. Current State Awareness: Where are you putting your energy and time right now? Create a detailed log of your activity.

3. Analysis and Alignment: Analyze your log with the areas you identified as being most important. Ask yourself where you want to *be* and put your actions in line with your priorities. Get support to help create your overtone balance.

*You can work through your own 'Alignment Log' in the *Overtone Effect Workbook.* See back page.

Chapter 25
ESTABLISHING PERSONAL BOUNDARIES

"Boundaries are an imaginary line of protection that you draw around you to protect your soul or what's important to you." [1]
—Thomas Leonard

To sustain our overtone, we need to be clear what our personal boundaries are and uphold them consistently. Boundaries come into play in all parts of our lives, and they change in different situations and relationships. The benefits of creating and honoring our personal boundaries are many. The most elemental purpose of boundaries is to keep us safe and protect us from harm. Respecting our boundaries puts us in the driver's seat and lets us control our destiny. Honoring our personal boundaries is a strong self-message that we are valuing ourselves.

The downside of not understanding what our boundaries are, or of not upholding them, includes stress, frustration, powerlessness, burnout, feeling like a victim, and more. Those negative emotions will interfere with sustaining an overtone.

If boundaries are so good why don't we consistently respect them? That's a complicated question. Probably the biggest reason is that setting and upholding boundaries is a risk. Others might not like our boundary and we could create conflict or affect relationships. Habitually, patterns may be so ingrained in some parts of our lives that to re-establish and re-clarify personal boundaries could be a tough slog.

We might even step over our own boundaries by overdoing our positive qualities thereby making them work against us. When we get attached to, stuck on, or over-rely on use of a particular strength, there can be some serious boundary-crossing repercussions. Over-committers, over-carers, and serial givers are a few examples of individuals who take a positive strength to extremes, which can cross personal boundaries and become negative.

One thing that particularly affects our ability to achieve a personal overtone is when we get mucked up about respecting our boundaries in the field of personal energy management. This is closely connected with the chapters on balance and resiliency – where and how we use our energy can greatly affect our capacity. Be sure to do the Energy Awareness exercise in Chapter 13 to see where your energy boundaries might be out of balance or in need of some tightening.

Identifying Personal Boundaries

In some areas of our lives, our boundaries can be clearly identified and described. Other areas will require more exploration. From a reactive position we can identify when a boundary has been crossed by paying attention to our emotional and physical feelings and to the things that push our buttons. When your triggered reaction is dramatic it's usually easy to trace back to the cause. It may take a bit more detective work to look back and see what triggered you when you experience more subtle feelings of discomfort or unease.

REFLECTION OPPORTUNITY

Look at four areas of your life – **physical, emotional, mental, and spiritual** – and think about your personal boundaries.

1. What are the personal boundaries you know you have in those four areas?
2. Which of those personal boundaries do you consistently honor?
3. Where and when do you not honor your boundaries?
4. How do you feel when you don't honor your boundaries?
5. What might need to shift for you to honor them?
6. What are the boundaries you would like to develop further?
7. Who can support you?

Chapter 26
CARING WITHOUT CARRYING

*"Letting go helps us to live in a more peaceful state of mind
and helps restore our balance. It allows others to be responsible for themselves, and for us to take our hands off situations that
do not belong to us. This frees us from unnecessary stress."* [1]
—Melody Beattie, best-selling self-help author

I remember prepping years ago for a four-month backpacking trip around
Europe. The *Lonely Planet Guidebook* was the youth travel gospel at the
time and it recommended laying out everything you wanted to take,
and then removing half of it. The guidebook said 50% of it was not needed
and we would sorely regret carrying around a heavy backpack. The same
principle applies to our lives. All the extra physical and mental stuff we carry
weighs us down, keeps us stuck, and gets in the way of our moving forward
into our overtone.

Emily teaches a group of high school students with developmental and
psychological challenges in the chronically underfunded public school
system. Her students demand more than a normal teaching curricu-
lum and resources can offer. Emily cares deeply about each of her students and feels 100% responsible for their learning. Yet it isn't possible
for her to give them the kind of specialized individual attention they
might need to really thrive. No matter how brilliant her teaching is, no
matter how much she gives, not all of her students are engaged. Emily
is frequently sleepless at night thinking of them, wishing she could do
more. She is experiencing the negative weight of responsibility and the
carrying of something outside her control. That "carrying" raises her

stress levels and affects her happiness. Learning how to "care without carrying" is something she is actively working on.

My coaching clients are generally an over-caring, high-achieving, over-committing bunch, and our coaching conversations often connect around a similar theme – that of being overwhelmed by the amount on their plates. Upon further conversation, we get at the real issue – it isn't the quantity on their plates that is overwhelming them, it is the feeling of being responsible for everything on their plates. Like Emily, they need to learn how to carry less without caring less.

When you begin examining this concept in the context of your own life, you may make some interesting discoveries. Let's first get clear on what we are responsible for and what we really do have to carry.

The Random House dictionary defines **Responsible** as *"Answerable or accountable, as for something within one's power or control."*

There are only four areas we can control or be fully responsible for:

1. **Our thoughts**
2. **Our intent**
3. **Our actions /behavior**
4. **Our words**

That's it. Simple, eh? We can care about everyone else's thoughts, behaviors, and what others say, but we are neither responsible for them, nor can we control them. Carrying them is both unnecessary and damaging. Letting them go will give us the critical space needed for our overtone to ring.

A Strength Overdone Can Be a Weakness

Keep in mind the discussion of the Strength Deployment Inventory (Chapter 8) and how a strength, if overdone (or perceived as being overdone), can be a weakness. Now let's take the desirable strength of caring. What might be the overdone interpretation of that beautiful strength? Possibly smothering, controlling, meddling, and submissive? By over-caring you might not only be doing yourself a disservice, but also you might inadvertently be doing a disservice to those you are caring for.

REFLECTION OPPORTUNITY

HOW TO CARRY LESS

Part One: Be Aware of the Load You Are Carrying

Looking through the lens of the four areas (thoughts, intention, actions, and words) consider the tasks, activities, and relationships in each area of your life.

First, write a list of the areas/tasks/activities/relationships in your life.

After you have created your list, ask yourself three questions:

1. What percentage responsibility do you feel for each of those areas/ activities listed?

2. What percentage do you have control over? (Remember, it is only possible to have 100% control over what you think, say, intend, and do)

3. How much do you care? (On a scale of 1–10)

Take a close look at your numbers. What do you notice?

Part Two: Separate the Carrying from the Caring

While still caring to the scaled level you identified for each area, figure out how you could carry less by cutting your percentage of mental responsibility in half. What would that mean in practical terms? This step might be purely a mental shift, yet it will require some tough personal talk and constant attention to make the shift.

Go through your list and make some "I will" statements that are a commitment to actions or new ways of thinking that will give you a responsibility break.

Do this exercise for your relationships as well. Which relationships feel weighty, are an energy drain, or are too complicated? Consider what you could do about those relationships to care, yet not carry. Could you step back? Set some boundaries? No longer engage in certain topics such as conflicts with others, repeated dramas, past wrongs, or perform certain roles such as rescuer, problem-solver, or counselor?

Reflect on what you are really responsible for. What could you let go of for both your own benefit and that of others?

Part Three: Making the Shift

Keep your focus on your 'Carry Less' Commitment column and imagine holding only 50% of the mental or physical responsibility that you do now. What might that feel like? Remind yourself that being less responsible does not have to affect your level of caring. Feel the freedom and empowerment that comes from intentionally deciding how much you want to carry.

CONTINUING THE CONVERSATION

Congratulations on working through this system to find, live in, and sustain your personal and organization overtone. I am honored that you have taken the time out of your busy lives to read my work.

Using the illustration of The Overtone System as a quick reference guide, let's recap our journey. We started with a foundation of values and guiding principles along with recognition of our strengths. We then moved into visioning our bright, bold, beautiful future. From there we dug a bit deeper to get at our *Why*, and we created our GPS (Guiding Purpose Slogan) to inspire us to move forward. We then expanded from micro to macro, starting with ourselves as individuals on our own lifelong journey to personal mastery. After that we looked at our role as leaders, which entailed how to *be* the leader and lead from wherever we stand.

We learned how to apply the concepts to the groups or organizations to which we belong. We then looked at some ways to help us work through barriers in order to be able to sustain our overtone. And the entire journey was fueled by a generative approach, with a generative mindset, and using generative language.

So now what? More of the same? Well, yes and no. There is more to do, but it is never the same! This is an ongoing journey, and an overtone can be fleeting. The happy part is that anyone can find his or her overtone – and the journey is where the gold is.

Here are a few ways to support your Overtone journey:

- Purchase the 70-page *Overtone Effect Workbook* in PDF format (instructions on the back page). In it you will find extensive resources and downloadable worksheets to help imbed your learning.
- Talk to me about speaking to your group or doing an *Overtone Effect* workshop.
- Visit my website www.creativecoachinggroup.com and sign up for a free subscription to my monthly e-newsletter filled with coaching articles.

Most of all I recommend putting some specific supports in place so that you can practice the principles and the system in this book. Having a coach or accountability partner will do more to propel you forward than any other initiative you might undertake. Plus, it's more fun!

I am here to support your overtone journey and I invite you to keep in touch. Feel free to email me at jan@creativecoachinggroup.com

Jan Carley

ELEVATOR RECAPS* AND TWITTER SUMMARIES**

* An Elevator Recap is a short summary for those quickie conversations that you might have on an elevator as you glide between floors

**Twitter posts are required to be a maximum of 140 characters

SECTION ONE

Beginning the Conversation Chapters 1–2

Twitter summary:

The overtone journey starts with you and a shift from DO HAVE BE to BE DO HAVE. An overtone requires total alignment and balance. #startwithin

SECTION TWO

The Overtone Approach Chapters 3–5

Generative Focus

Elevator Recap:

The overtone approach is a generative one, which means a life-giving, action oriented, energy-filled, and forward-moving focus. Positive thinking is a start. We then need to increase our positivity ratio and go even further to move into action. The overtone approach has us focus our minds in a toward state, one in which we focus on what we want and where we want to go. When we get mired in the scarcity thinking of "what isn't working" and "what we don't want" we can remind ourselves to get into a generative mindset by two simple words: "Flip it!" Weaknesses are opportunities for change and improvement.

Twitter Summary:

A generative focus is life-giving. Keep your mind on what you want, instead of what you don't want to open up your possibilities. #flipit

Generative Mindset

Elevator Recap:

To find our overtone we must adopt a growth mindset. Our brains support the concept that what we focus on, we will see. By showing up as a learner, staying curious, and relaxing the knowing muscle, we open opportunities. Moving from self-judgment to self-assessment keeps our mental space open. Self-assessment is an objective process where we notice, evaluate, build on, and move to what we want. Judgment shuts us down, and we need open space to find our overtone.

Twitter Summary:

What we focus on is what we will see. To find our overtone we must adopt a learning, growth mindset that is judgment-free. #brainpower

Generative Language

Elevator Recap:

Even a single word in a sentence has the power to shift us from generative and forward-moving to stalled or even damaging. Words create a physiological response. We want to use words that will keep our brains in a toward state. Use language to open possibilities, to create choice. Don't say, "Don't!" Keep the scene going by saying "Yes, and…" Where thought goes, energy flows.

Twitter Summary:

Even a single word has the power to vault us forward or shut us down. Use language to keep brains in a toward state. #dontsaydont

SECTION THREE

Building the Overtone Foundation Chapters 6–11

Elevator Recap:

Each building block of your overtone foundation is important. Defining your personal and organizational values is the critical first step. Values act as drivers, influencers, guides, course correctors, decision makers, and supports. Determining guiding principles linked with your values will powerfully amplify your overtone.

Building from there to identify, work from, and optimize your strengths will accelerate your success. Add your vision – your beacon and North Star – and imagine your greatest possibilities. The impossible *is* possible! Determine your *Why* – the emotional element that drives your vision. Create a GPS (Guiding Purpose Slogan) to constantly inspire you.

Twitter Summary:
Build a solid overtone foundation with identification of values, guiding principles, strengths, vision, your *Why*, and GPS. #startwithvalues

SECTION FOUR

Creating Your Personal Overtone Chapters 12–14

Elevator Recap:
Personal mastery is all about the journey. It begins with an intentional creation of your personal mastery plan – defining where you are, establishing a vision of where you want to go, and challenging and stretching yourself to live into that vision.

Honoring and valuing your own needs allows you to show up fully in the world. Self-care is not selfishness. It is the way you will be able to find and stay in your overtone and contribute the most to the world. Remember the oxygen mask – it's impossible to take care of others if you don't take care of yourself first.

You can form a new self-talk habit and move from self-criticism to self-acceptance to open your overtone path. Limiting beliefs are, well, *limiting*! Take control of the voices in your head and turn them from critics to helpful coaches.

Twitter Summary:
Personal mastery is a holistic journey. Taking care of yourself will help you contribute more fully to others. #putyourownoxygenmaskonfirst

SECTION FIVE
Overtone Leadership Chapters 15–18

Being the Leader

Elevator Recap:

Leadership is less a set of skills or a role than a way of being. You can be a leader if you show up and authentically and act from that place of congruency. How to be a leader? Commit to the personal mastery journey – that is the most powerful influencer. You must *be* the change. Walk the talk and model the behavior you want to create a strong foundation of trust. Leaders with charisma draw out the best in others. Overtone leaders operate with a growth mindset and lead with intention. (Oh, yes – vulnerability is okay)

Twitter Summary:

Overtone leaders walk the talk and lead with intention. Modeling commitment to growth and mastery is a powerful influence. #walkthetalk

Role of a Leader

Elevator Recap:

The role of a leader is to create an environment where the individual talents of the team can flourish and shine to their full potential. Overtone leaders show up in their full authentic self, and then go beyond self to create the conditions for others to grow and thrive. They aren't "making" it happen – they are creating the space for the overtone to happen.

Intrinsic Inspiration

Elevator Recap:

Intrinsic inspiration builds from an aligned place of connection to self and is a burning fire that refuels from within. External motivation is great for the short term. For longer-lasting effects, invite change instead of imposing it. Turn obligations into opportunities and feel the energy shift. For a sustainable possibility of working in our overtone we want to shift from negative external motivation to positive internal inspiration.

There will always be a *Bitsy Fairhaven*

Elevator Recap:

Bitsy represents the up-to-20% who simply don't get on board. Bitsy can derail us as leaders. It's your choice how you deal with your Bitsy. In this chapter we learned a few options including giving Bitsy an MRI (Most Respectful Interpretation), holding to our foundation of values and choosing our focus.

Overtone Leadership

Twitter Summary:

Overtone leaders intentionally create conditions for others to thrive. They allow space for an overtone to happen. #anovertonecantbeimposed

SECTION SIX

Overtones for Organizations Chapters 19–22

Elevator Recap:

Discover your differentiators as an organization and what makes you unique. If you aren't in tune with your organization's "sound," it could be working against you. Do the work of defining your foundational elements and build from there. Be purposeful and intentional and patient. It can take three to five years for a full culture shift or revitalization. There must be a baseline willingness for any organization to make a shift. Finding your organization overtone is an ever changing, flexible process that will need to be revisited and adapted on a regular basis. Support your overtone by practicing how to give deep acknowledgment. Adopt the generative practice of Feed Forward to have a mutual exchange about growth opportunities.

Twitter Summary:

Discover your org's differentiating sound and build the overtone foundation from there. Be intentional and patient. #romewasntbuiltinaday

SECTION SEVEN

Sustaining the Overtone Chapters 23–26

Elevator Recap:

Creating an overtone is a delicate endeavor that can be thrown off by a host of external and internal factors. Though challenging to sustain, a strong foundation will make it easier to find and live in your overtone more often. Some of the common challenges to sustaining an overtone are discussed from a generative perspective in this section. Building resiliency capacity, creating balance, establishing boundaries, and "caring without carrying" will help create the space for your overtone to flourish.

Twitter Summary:

An overtone is easily quashed. Resiliency, balance, boundaries and caring without carrying help your overtone flourish. #strongfoundation

ACKNOWLEDGMENTS

I have been inspired and supported by so many in the writing of this book. My heartfelt gratitude goes out to all my clients, who share their work and lives with me every day, and whose stories are threaded through this book. Working with you has made my life so rich.

Thank you to my coaching colleagues, who have given themselves to making the world a better place and whose work continues to fuel and support me. Thanks also to those who have allowed me to use their quotes and content in this book. I encourage you to visit their websites listed in the resource section, and to read their books.

Thanks to all of those who generously contributed their stories, ideas, inspiration and/or who gave feed forward as one of my beta readers in the editing of this book: Sue Averill, Marc Bowles, Britt-Heléne Bonnedahl and the Rönninge Show Chorus, Joy Bruce, Marj Busse, Dave Carley, Gord Carley, Carollyne Conlinn, Sarah Evans, Meghan Fell, Brian Fraser, Nancy Fulton, Cindy Gauthier, Stephanie Hardman, Shannon Harris, Becki Hine and the Song of Atlanta Show Chorus, Amanda Hunt, Cammi and Don MacKinlay, Lesley-Ann Marriott, Sandy Marron and the Lions Gate Chorus, Donya Metzger, David Mollenhauer, Steven Moyes, Nancy Mudford, Louise Owen, Region 6 SAI, Chris Temperante, and Volkart May.

Thanks to Yvonne Meyer of Meyer Print Graphics for the contribution of graphics in the book, to Sam Bradd for his awesome illustration of The Overtone System, and Glenda MacFarlane for her editing savvy. My extreme gratitude to Joy Bruce, who generously answered my call for help with the proofreading process, even sacrificing part of her vacation to help me meet my deadline.

Special thanks to my brother, Dave, for his incredibly valuable writing advice and ongoing guidance. I give several high fives to my writing account-ability partner, CD, and our BKWRs (Butt Kicking Writers Retreats), without which I don't think I would ever have completed this book.

Lastly, thanks to my coach(es), to Liam and Riki-lea, and to my Lions Gate Chorus singing family for their constant support and belief in me.

P.S. I would be remiss if I didn't make special mention of the external aid of "Crackles," a trusted recipe handed down through generations that served as my tightly-crafted reward system throughout the writing process (recipe below).

<u>Crackles</u>
I cup brown sugar
3 cups Quick Quaker Oats
½ pound melted butter

Mix together and pat down firmly into an 8-inch square pan.
Bake at 325°-350°F for 20 to 25 minutes, or until golden
brown on top. Cool before cutting (if you can wait that long!)
and treat yourself after every block of completed writing.

ENDNOTES

Chapter 1 What is an Overtone?
1. Shannon Harris is a two-time International Quartet champion; Brava! 2004 and Martini 2012 www.martiniquartet.com

Chapter 2 How to Create an Overtone
1. Neale Donald Walsch, Author of *Conversations with God*, www.nealedonaldwalsch.com

Chapter 3 Generative Focus
1. Fredrickson, B. L. (2013, July 15). Updated Thinking on Positivity Ratios. *American Psychologist*. Advance online publication. doi: 10.1037/a0033584, p.3,7. I was originally inspired by Dr. Barbara Fredrickson's seminal book, *Positivity* (New York: Crown Publishers, 2009).
2. Shawn Achor, The Happiness Advantage (New York: Crown Business, 2010), 44.
3. The organizational approach of Appreciative Inquiry (AI) is creating a positive revolution in the leadership of change. http://appreciativeinquiry.case.edu
4. Cooperrider, David L.;Whitney, Diana; and Stavros, Jacqueline M., *Appreciative Inquiry Handbook: The First in a Series of AI Workbooks for Leaders of Change* (Lakeshore Communications, 2003), XVII-XIX.
5. Cooperrider, D.L. et al. (Eds.), *Lessons from the Field: Applying Appreciative Inquiry* (Thin Book Publishing, 2001), 12.
6. Volkart May www.volkartmay.com
7. Dr. David Rock, author and co-founder of the Neuroleadership Institute and Summit talks extensively about the brain's toward and away responses. Detailed insights in his book, *Your Brain at Work* (New York: HarperCollins Publishers, 2009), 105. www.neuroleadership.org
8. C. Otto Scharmer, "Uncovering the Blind Spot of Leadership" (*Leader to Leader*, 47 Winter 2008), 54.
9. Jacqueline M. Stavros and Gina Hinrichs, *Thin Book of SOAR: Building Strengths-Based Strategy* (Thin Book Publishing Co; 2009), www.soar-strategy.com
10. Region 6 SAI www.regionsix.org

Chapter 4 Generative Mindset
1. Dr. Michael M. Merzenich is a world-renowned neuroscientist who has been a leading pioneer in brain plasticity research for nearly five decades. Author of Soft-Wired: How the New Science of Brain Plasticity Can Change Your Life. www.onthebrain.com
2. Dr. Carol Dweck, *Mindset – The New Psychology of Success* (New York: Random House, 2007). Dr. Dweck is a world-renowned Stanford University psychologist and one of the world's leading researchers in the field of motivation. www.mindsetonline.com

3. Royal Roads University Graduate Certificate in Executive Coaching Program. www. royalroads.ca
4. Rosamund Stone Zander and Benjamin Zander, *The Art of Possibility* (New York: Penguin Books, 2002), 31.
5. Dr. Adam McLeod, "Using Intentions in Healing" (*Canadian Journal of Reflexology*, March 2011, Vol. 5, Issue 2), 4. Known as Dreamhealer, Dr. McLeod brings a scientific framework to healing with intentions. www.dreamhealer.com

Chapter 5 Generative Language
1. The two question experiment was introduced by Sarah Evans, Ph.D. (c), PCC, in the Royal Roads University Foundations of Executive Coaching Course webinar series.
2. The 'Get to Do' list originated from Amy Ahlers and Christine Arylo, co-founders of the Inner Mean Girl Reform School www.wakeupcallcoaching.com

Chapter 6 The Value of Values
1. John G. Blumberg, author of *Return on Integrity* www.BlumbergROI.com

Chapter 8 Maximizing Strengths
1. Tom Rath, *StrengthsFinder 2.0* (New York: Gallup Press, 2007), i.
2. Lions Gate Chorus www.lionsgatechorus.ca
3. Dr. Donald O. Clifton, (1924-2003) creator of the Clifton StrengthsFinder®, was named the Father of Strengths-Based Psychology by an American Psychological Association Presidential Commendation 2002. *StrengthsFinder 2.0* (New York: Gallup Press, 2007), i.
4. Rönninge Show Chorus www.ronningeshow.com
5. Dr. Seuss, *Happy Birthday to You!* (New York: Random House books for Young Readers, 1959).
6. Rath, StrengthsFinder 2.0, iii.
7. Strength Deployment Inventory®, SDI® and Relationship Awareness Theory® are Registered Trademarks of PSP Inc., Carlsbad, CA

Chapter 9 Vision: Thinking Outside the Dot
1. Robert Fritz, *The Path of Least Resistance* (New York: Fawcett-Columbine, 1989).
2. Carl Jung (1875-1961), Swiss psychiatrist and psychotherapist
3. Stone Zander and Zander, *The Art of Possibility*, 169-170

Chapter 10 What is your Why?
1. Simon Sinek, TED talk: "How Great Leaders Inspire Action," 2009; Book: *Start with WHY*

Section 4 Introduction
1. Kevin Cashman, *Leadership from the Inside Out* (San Francisco: Berrett-Koehler Publishers, Inc., 2008), 34.

Chapter 12 Personal Mastery
1. Leo Tolstoy (1828-1910), Russian writer
2. Malcolm Gladwell, *Outliers* (New York: Back Bay Books/Little, Brown and Company, 2008), 35.
3. Peter Senge, *The Fifth Discipline* (New York: Doubleday, 2006), 131.
4. The International Coach Federation (ICF) is the world's leading professional association for coaches with over 20,000 coaches in 100 countries worldwide. www.coachfederation.org
5. Marjorie Busse, MCC Essential Impact Inc. www.essentialimpact.com
6. Cashman, *Leadership from the Inside Out*, 37.
7. Senge, *The Fifth Discipline*, 132.
8. T.S. Eliot (1888-1965), Playwright, poet

Chapter 14 Self-Talk
1. My mom, Margaret Carley (1924-2015), always had amazing words of wisdom. This nugget was given in her 90th year.
2. Rock, *Your Brain at Work*, 106.
3. Louise Hay is author and founder of Hay House, Inc., the international leader in inspirational and self-help publishing. I have had my set of Louise Hay affirmation cards since 1990 and I use them every day! www.louisehay.com
4. Dr. Brené Brown, *The Gifts of Imperfection* (Center City: Hazeldon Publishing, 2010). Her TED talk – The Power of Vulnerability- is one of the top five most viewed TED talks in the world with over twenty-five million views
5. Gladys Edmunds, Author, Business consultant, speaker www.gladysedmunds.com
6. Albert Einstein (1879-1955), German-born physicist

Section 5 Introduction
1. Cashman, *Leadership from the Inside Out*, 83.

Chapter 15 *Being* the Leader
1. Michael Stratford, MCC uses the *Being* as the starting point for all his leadership work www.michaelstratford.com
2. Senge, *The Fifth Discipline*, 162.
3. Eleanor Roosevelt (1884-1962), longest-serving First Lady of the United States, diplomat and activist

Chapter 16 The Role of a Leader Simplified
1. Denis Waitley, Ph.D, best-selling author, speaker and success coach, quote from *The Denis Waitley ezine*, March 2, 2005, Issue 22. www.deniswaitley.com

Chapter 17 Intrinsic Inspiration
1. Bob Nelson, Ph.D, best-selling author, *1501 Ways to Reward Employees* www.drbobnelson.com

2. Daniel H. Pink, *DRIVE - The Surprising Truth About What Motivates Us* (New York: Penguin Group, 2009), 218-219. www.danpink.com

3. Thomas J. Leonard is known as the founding father of professional coaching. He was founder, in 1992 of Coach U – the first school for professional life coaches. He also founded, in 1994, the International Coach Federation. In 2000 he founded CoachVille.com. For more information, visit www.BestofThomas.com

4. Pink, *DRIVE -The Surprising Truth About What Motivates Us*, 218.

Chapter 18 There Will Always Be a *Bitsy Fairhaven*

1. Shaun Belding, CEO, The Belding Group of Companies, www.beldingtraining.com

2. The MRI (Most Respectful Interpretation) used with permission from Dr. John J. Scherer, www.WiserAtWork.com www.SchererCenter.com

Chapter 19 The Sound of your Organization

1. Ludwig van Beethoven (1770-1827), German composer

Chapter 20 Culture by Design

1. Dr. Carol Dweck's growth and fixed mindset concepts are detailed in her book, *Mindset – The New Psychology of Success* (New York: Random House, 2007). www.mindsetonline.com

2. Song of Atlanta Show Chorus. www.songofatlanta.com

3. Janet Harvey, MCC, "Coaching from Full Potential" (*Choice* - The Magazine of Professional Coaching, Vol 13, Number 3), 21. www.invitechange.com

4. Carollyne Conlinn, MCC Essential Impact Inc. www.essentialimpact.com

Chapter 21 Creating an Acknowledgment Rich Culture

1. Dr. Paul White, International Expert on workplace relationships, Author of *Employee Recognition that Works: Using the 5 Languages of Appreciation to Build a Positive Work Environment*, speaker at WBECS Webinar June 26, 2015. www.appreciationatwork.com

2. H. Jackson Brown Jr., Author, *Life's Little Instruction Book: 511 Suggestions, Observations, and Reminders on How to Live a Happy and Rewarding Life.* www.instructionbook.com

3. www.BestofThomas.com

Chapter 22 Generative Growth Through Feed Forward

1. Marshall Goldsmith, Try feedforward instead of feedback. (Adapted from Leader to Leader, 25 Summer 2002), 11-14. Dr. Goldsmith is a world-renowned business educator, coach and best-selling author of *What Got You Here Won't Get You There.* www.marshallgoldsmith.com

2. Dr. Marcia Reynolds, MCC, best-selling author of *The Discomfort Zone: How Leaders Turn Difficult Conversations into Breakthroughs* www.outsmartyourbrain.com

Chapter 23 Building Resiliency

1. Michael Jordan, Former NBA superstar, BrainyQuote.com, XploreInc, 2016. http://www.brainyquote.com/quotes/quotes/m/michaeljor127660.html
2. The story of Perdita Felicien was part of my first book, and I felt it had such a compelling message around resiliency that it needed to be included in this book. *Harmony from the Inside Out* (Creative Coaching Group Publishing, 2009), 132.
3. Paul Boese (1923-1976), Kansas businessman and author of inspirational quotes.
4. Georgia O'Keeffe (1887-1986), American artist

Chapter 24 Creating Balance

1. Learn more about Kent Avery's balancing rocks on his Facebook page "The Art of Balance" by Kent Avery
2. Joan Gurvis, *Leadership in the Balance – Balancing Act: Shifting to Find Equilibrium* (Center for Creative Leadership – CCL e-newsletter Sept. 2007).

Chapter 25 Establishing Personal Boundaries

1. www.BestofThomas.com

Chapter 26 Caring without Carrying

1. Melody Beattie, best-selling self-help author. www.melodybeattie.com

RESOURCES AND RECOMMENDED WEBSITES

The following people and their works inspired or contributed to the content or production of this book. I encourage you to visit their websites and support their work.

Shawn Achor - *The Happiness Advantage* - www.shawnachor.com

The Appreciative Inquiry Commons - a worldwide portal to share information on Appreciative Inquiry and the rapidly growing discipline of positive change. http://appreciativeinquiry.case.edu

Melody Beattie - www.melodybeattie.com

Shaun Belding - www.beldingtraining.com

John G. Blumberg – www.BlumbergROI.com

Sam Bradd - www.drawingoutsidethelines.com

Brené Brown – *The Gifts of Imperfection* and TED Talk: The Power of Vulnerability www.courageworks.com/about/brene-brown

H. Jackson Brown Jr. – *Life's Little Instruction Book: 511 Suggestions, Observations, and Reminders on How to Live a Happy and Rewarding Life*. www.instructionbook.com

Marjorie Busse - Essential Impact Coaching Inc. - www.essentialimpact.com

Kevin Cashman - *Leadership from the Inside Out* - www.cashmanleadership.com

CHOICE – The Magazine of Professional Coaching – www.choice-online.com

Clifton StrengthsFinder 2.0 assessment - www.strengthsfinder.com

Carollyne Conlinn - Essential Impact Coaching Inc. - www.essentialimpact.com

Dr. David Cooperrider - www.davidcooperrider.com

Dr. Carol Dweck - *Mindset – The New Psychology of Success* - www.mindsetonline.com

Fandango Quartet - www.fandangoquartet.com

Perdita Felicien - www.perditafelicien.com

Dr. Barbara L. Fredrickson – *Positivity* - http://www.positivityratio.com

Dr. Marshall Goldsmith – *What Got You Here Won't Get You There* - www.marshallgoldsmith.com

Joan Gurvis – co-author, *Finding Your Balance* - www.insights.ccl.org/people

Shannon Harris and Martini Quartet - www.martiniquartet.com

Janet Harvey - www.invitechange.com

Louise L. Hay - www.louisehay.com

Thomas Leonard - www.bestofthomas.com

Lions Gate Chorus - www.lionsgatechorus.ca

Dr. Adam McLeod - www.dreamhealer.com

Lesley-Ann Marriott – www.marriottmanagement.ca

Dr. Michael Merzenich - www.onthebrain.com

Meyer Print Graphics - www.meyerprintgraphics.com

Dr. Bob Nelson - www.drbobnelson.com

Daniel Pink - *Drive – The Surprising Truth about What Motivates Us* – www.danpink.com

Tom Rath - Strengthsfinder 2.0 - www.tomrath.org

Region 6 SAI - www.regionsix.org

Dr. Marcia Reynolds – *The Discomfort Zone: How Leaders Turn Difficult Conversations into Breakthroughs* - www.outsmartyourbrain.com

Dr. David Rock - *Your Brain at Work* - www.neuroleadership.org

Rönninge Show Chorus - www.ronningeshow.com

Dr. C. Otto Scharmer - www.ottoscharmer.com

Dr. John J. Scherer - www.WiserAtWork.com - www.SchererCenter.com

Peter Senge - *The Fifth Discipline – The Art and Practice of the Learning Organization* – www.solonline.org

Simon Sinek - www.startwithwhy.com

Song of Atlanta Show Chorus - www.songofatlanta.com

Jacqueline M. Stavros and Gina Hinrichs, *Thin Book of SOAR*, www.thinbook.com

Strength Deployment Inventory® - www.totalsdi.com

Michael Stratford - www.michaelstratford.com

Denis Waitley - www.deniswaitley.com

Neale Donald Walsch - www.nealedonaldwalsch.com

Dr. Paul White - www.appreciationatwork.com

Rosamund and Benjamin Zander - *The Art of Possibility* - www.benjaminzander.com

ALSO BY JAN CARLEY

HARMONY FROM THE INSIDE OUT
Creating and Maximizing Your Performance Potential

I nspired by the extensive coaching work Jan has done with high-level a cappella choruses worldwide, *Harmony from the Inside Out* is powerfully insightful and filled with practical concepts and exercises that will shift limiting paradigms and instantly open up infinite possibilities for your work, your team, and your life. Includes a bonus 50-page action guide download.

Praise was unanimous for *Harmony from the Inside Out*:

"Jan is Canada's Ben Zander (*The Art of Possibility*). She has taken sound coaching principles, tested them on hundreds of women singers in competitive a cappella choruses, and created easily applied principles so that anyone can begin to maximize their potential." —Carollyne Conlinn, 2009 Canadian Coach of the Year

"These inner coaching principles will change you and your chorus culture (or any team you might work with) forever." —Sandy Marron, Master 700 Director, Lions Gate Chorus, 2016 International 5th Place Medalists

"I highly recommend Jan Carley's *Harmony from the Inside Out*. Jan has put together a fascinating approach to achieving your full potential." —Dr. John J. Scherer, Author, *5 Questions that Change Everything*

"This book is a MUST read for every leader, director and coach who wants his/her chorus to have a peak performance, not only on stage but at every rehearsal. — Britt-Heléne Bonnedahl, Master 700 Director, 2014 & 2017 International Gold Medalist Champions, Rönninge Show Chorus, Sweden

"Jan does a great job of taking the 'Inner Game of Music' theory and blending it with other behavioral and psychological theories to come up with a unique perspective on realizing your full potential. Highly recommended." — Kevin Keller, Past Chairman, Barbershop Harmony Society Contest and Judging Committee

ONLINE BOOK ORDERS:
www.harmonyfromtheinsideout.com
BULK ORDERS WITH DISCOUNTS
are available:
email: jan@creativecoachinggroup.com

STRENGTH DEPLOYMENT TRAINING
WITH JAN CARLEY

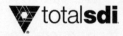

THE SDI – UNDERSTANDING MOTIVATION

The SDI® (Strength Deployment Inventory®) is the flagship learning resource of a suite of leadership and organizational development tools based on the theory of Relationship Awareness (RA). The full suite of RA assessments includes eight valid and reliable tools that work together to generate awareness of self and others; provide perceptive feedback; and, clarify expectations in work roles and relationships.

The SDI® is a proven, memorable tool for improving individual and team effectiveness. It is a learning model for effectively and accurately understanding the motives behind behavior. When people recognize the unique motivation of themselves and others – both when things are going well or not so well – they greatly enhance their ability to communicate more effectively and handle conflict more productively.

For individuals, this will result in more effective relationships and better communication with business colleagues or employees. It will also enhance personal relationships with life partners, friends and family. For teams and staff groups, this tool and its accompanying workshop can begin the awareness, understanding, and conversations that will aid in developing open communication and understanding, create more productive and happier relationships, and shift teams to be more fully-functional and living into their peak potential. www.totalsdi.com

Contact Jan Carley
jan@creativecoachinggroup.com
for information on full or half-day
workshops for groups from 5 to100
or the SDI® package for couples

ABOUT THE AUTHOR

Jan Carley is a professional certified executive coach, credentialed with the International Coach Federation. She specializes in coaching high-achieving executives and teams to clarify their vision and leverage their signature strengths to maximize their performance potential. Jan draws on her more than twenty-five years of experience working in executive positions in the professional non-profit world of the performing arts to bring a progressive whole-brained approach to her coaching programs. Challenging her clients to smash limiting paradigms that are barriers to their success and supporting them as they create transformative new possibilities, has made Jan a sought-after coach globally.

Jan is currently Associate Faculty at Royal Roads University, where she teaches the coaching foundations and personal mastery components of the university's prestigious Executive Coaching Program. Jan has also established an important niche as the "Inner Coach of Barbershop." In that role she has inspired dozens of internationally competitive a cappella choruses, their leadership teams, and thousands of singers worldwide to shift and expand their mindsets and operating cultures to ones of positivity, possibility, and excellence, and consequently, achieve significant performance results as they prepare for the pressured demands of international singing competitions.

Jan lives in Vancouver, BC, Canada, and is available for individual or group coaching, workshops, and speaking engagements worldwide.

www.creativecoachinggroup.com

**Bulk Book Order discounts are available –
email: jan@creativecoachinggroup.com**

THE OVERTONE EFFECT
WORKBOOK DOWNLOAD

(70 pages of downloadable worksheets and exercises in PDF format to support the concepts in the book)

Printed in Canada